THE BAREFOOT HIKER

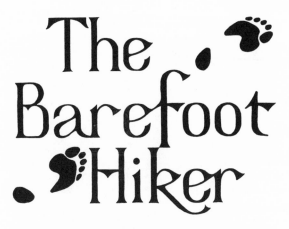

The Barefoot Hiker

A Book About Bare Feet

and how their sensitivity can provide not only
an unique dimension of pleasure, but also significant
benefits in safety, comfort, and confidence to hikers
who learn to rely upon them.

Richard Keith Frazine, B.D.

founder of the Barefoot Hikers
of Thomaston, Connecticut

TEN SPEED PRESS
BERKELEY, CALIFORNIA

"Shoeless in the Forest" by Liz Halloran, September 15, 1991, is reprinted by permission of the Waterbury Republican-American, Waterbury, Connecticut.

1☉

Ten Speed Press
P.O. Box 7123
Berkeley, California 94707

Cover design by Fifth Street Design
Text design by Sarah Levin
Cover photograph of the author and son Charles leading a barefoot hike along the Mattatuck Trail. Taken by the Rev. Dr. Raymond Odiorne, Jr.
Chapter opening photographs of forest floor by Sara Glaser.

Library of Congress Cataloging-in-Publication Data
   Frazine, Richard Keith.
    The barefoot hiker: a book about bare feet /
  Richard Keith Frazine
    ISBN 0-89815-525-8
    1. Hiking. 2. Foot. I. Title.
  GV199.5.F73   1993
  796.5'2—dc20   92-34756
                             CIP

FIRST PRINTING 1993
Printed in the United States of America
1 2 3 4 5 — 97 96 95 94 93

A Note of Thanks

To Judith, Thia, and Kate Odiorne, and to Sue Smith for their extensive help in the preparation of this book, both as friends and fellow writers, and as participants in the barefoot hiking program whereupon the book is based.

To my agent, John White, at whose behest I began this project, for his unstinting help and encouragement at every stage of it.

To my wife and family for their encouragement and support, on and off the trail.

To the many journalists who have freely and willingly cooperated with the Barefoot Hikers of Thomaston to make our program a success.

To the many barefoot hikers whom I have known over the years, and especially the many first-time barefoot hikers whose confidence in my abilities as a teacher has allowed me to develop those abilities to the point where I could, in confidence, begin this book.

To the aforementioned Odiornes, my own Beth and Charlie, Jason Hubbard, and Tim Quaranta for turning out, bravely barefoot and otherwise in uniform, despite unexpectedly cold weather on the day we did the cover photography.

BARE FEET THE FOREST FLOOR BEFRIENDING
FOLLOW DEFTLY DOWN SOME DEERPATH
SOFTLY STEPPING SOLEBARE SILENCE
SELDOM BREAKING BAREFOOT WALK
THE WISE IN WOODCRAFT WILLBENT EARTHBEARN
BOUNDS BENIGHTING BREAK BENEATH THEM
NOW TO KNOW WITH KINDRED KNOWING
KINDS THAT BUILT BEFORE THE BUILDERS
THINGS THE THOUGHTFULL THOUGHT UNTHINKING
THOUGH WITH WISDOM WONDROUS WROUGHT
FEELING FAVOUR'D YET TO FEEL SUCH
THINGS THE SHOD HAD SHUN'D LEST SHOELESS
THEY SHOULD TOUCH WHAT THEY'D ATTAINTED
TELLING FAIR THINGS FELL AND FOUL
THINGS THE BAREFOOT BLESS AS BEING
GODWORK GIVEN GRACE TO GREET
BARE FEET

Table of Contents

INTRODUCTION

How I Came to Write This Book

This book had its conception, as it were, late in the autumn of 1988. I was hiking with a Sierra Club group in Western Connecticut. A lady hiker in the group asked me about my bare feet. Her questions were polite, sincere, and searching. They were typical of those that countless people had asked me over nearly twenty years of barefoot hiking. What she really wanted to know was what it *felt* like to go barefoot along a forest trail. She wanted to know about the leaves, the pine needles, the moss-covered rocks, and the rich, dark earth. It was like being asked what something tasted like. All I could tell her was that the sensations she was asking about were very pleasant; some of them were nothing short of delicious; but to know them one simply had to go barefoot. I could sense a mixture of envy and fearful reserve. It was time to tell her what another barefoot hiker had once told me, when I had stood, still shod, on the edge of wanting to go barefoot: "Take off your shoes."

No. The time was not right. It was just a little too cold. She would though. In the summer maybe.

I felt badly because I knew how much she would have enjoyed it. I suppose I was also a bit disappointed at the loss of an opportunity to share something that meant a great deal to me.

As we parted company at the end of the walk, the leader, and in fact "group chair," Trisha Ashcroft, introduced herself to me. She wanted to know if I would be willing to lead a series of barefoot hikes along the Mattatuck Trail the next spring. I was quite pleased with the idea.

I took my preparation for the project very seriously. I had, in the past, on a few odd occasions, the opportunity to share the experience of going barefoot with someone or other whom I might have met on the trail. This, however, would be different. There would be at least a dozen people, most of them barefoot for the very first time, and I would have to teach them all to go barefoot safely. I felt a genuine responsibility and I wanted to make the best job of it that I could. I saw a need to be able to give participants something that they could take home with them and study; something that would cover, in a well thought out way, all the points that I would have liked to make but was all too likely to forget in the course of leading a hike.

I would have been quite content simply to photocopy a few pages of some book or article on the subject of barefoot hiking, but there was simply nothing available anywhere. I had certainly looked. Over the years I had made a habit of checking and asking in every book shop, library, and nature center* that I came across in my travels throughout England and North America; but although I found the footprints (both real and metaphorical) of a number of barefoot hikers, I never found anything that had ever actually been published on the subject, not even so much as a brief article. This was especially frustrating because at least two of the barefoot hikers whom I had met or heard about had published works on other outdoor themes. Still, I persevered. I made inquiries to the Ramblers Association, the Audubon Society, the Sierra Club, the Appalachian Trail Council, and other like organizations, but found no help in my search. Needless to say, I checked through past and present editions of *Books in Print* and the *Readers' Guide to Periodical Literature*, but again to no avail. My search would not have been complete without an investigation of what various books on hiking, walking, woodcraft, wilderness survival, and other related topics had to say on the subject. I do not pretend that I have made a totally exhaustive search in this area, but I have devoted many hours of library time to making at least an index search of as many books as I have come across whose titles and formats even suggested that they might make some reference to barefoot hiking. I read every page

---

*I would not like anyone to suppose that the Websterian spellings in this book are my own. I would have written "centre," in accordance with Oxford Dictionary usage. It was decided, however, to apply the occasionally different standards of Mr. Webster, as it was thought that these would be more familiar, and thus less distracting, to a larger number of readers, particularly in North America.—R.K.F.

that I found indexed not only under "feet" or "going barefoot" but also under shoes, footwear, clothing, equipment, and various other headings. I also took the time to thumb through many unindexed books. One or two contained a sentence or so expressing hostility to the idea. One or two more cautiously allowed that going barefoot might be appropriate along beaches but gave no more space to it. The vast majority contained no mention of bare feet at all. What saddened me the most was that two or three books in this last and largest class had photographs showing their authors barefoot in several shots. If they enjoyed going barefoot, why could they not have shared this with their readers?

Knowing from all of this fruitless research that if I were going to be able to hand out a booklet on barefoot hiking, I would have to write it myself, I sat down to do so. The result was a small pamphlet the length of which I carefully kept to eight single spaced letter size pages, so that when reduced down to half size, it would fit on the two sides of a single sheet of paper. In addition to providing a full size copy to every first time barefoot hiker who came out with us, I could thus economically fold minuscule copies in with our hiking club handouts and continually replenish stacks of these at half a dozen locations within as many miles of my home in Thomaston, Connecticut. I have had to run off several dozen each month to keep up with only this very local demand.

Until an article on the Barefoot Hikers by Francis Chamberlain appeared in *The New York Times* in September of 1991, it was virtually impossible for me to share anything about barefoot hiking with anyone beyond perhaps a thirty-mile radius of my home in

Thomaston. It is my hope that this book will change that and allow me to encourage people all across North America (and hopefully some of the rest of the English-speaking world as well) to take up barefoot hiking. I would further hope that some few of those might find the energy and determination to establish groups in other places with regular barefoot hiking programs such as ours here in Thomaston. Those who do will be providing something really enjoyable for a great many others.

Going barefoot in the forest is a very sensuous and pleasurable experience. For some of us it is almost a mystical experience. I know that I dreamt of it long before I ever dared try it. It is also an experience that brings into question our entire relationship with nature in a way that disturbs and challenges our ideas about ourselves as civilized beings. It is an experience that I have long wanted to see explored properly in print.

CHAPTER 1

How We Feel
About Bare Feet

A Typical Telephone Conversation

"What does 'barefoot' mean?"

"We hike in our bare feet."

"Oh…I thought it was just a *name*—for some sort of 'back-to-nature' thing—not people actually going *barefoot!*"

Curious as this bit of conversation seems, I can tell you that something like this occurs in most of the dozens of telephone calls that I receive each season in response to press notices for the Barefoot Hikers of Thomaston, Connecticut; and that in most of the others, it turns out that the caller has managed not to read the word "barefoot" in the notice at all. I have never fully understood why this one simple word should be the subject of such constant and consistent misunderstanding.

One thought that occurs to me is that while, in a *remote* sense, the word "barefoot" conjures up pleasant, romantic images of a simpler and more innocent age; when taken in the *immediate* sense for most people, the idea of walking through the woods unshod is somehow so disturbing that they manage to either mentally delete it from the text, or consign it to the safe and pleasant realm of romantic metaphor. Nevertheless, most of those who stumble over the word "barefoot" in just such a way are, in the end, game enough to come out with us and find that they enjoy the actual experience of going barefoot themselves. Maybe they manage to step into that remote romantic image when they take off their shoes. Maybe they overcome the fears that made the immediate sense of the word so disturbing. In any case, our feelings, both romantic and fearful, both about the word "barefoot" and the bare fact of bare feet are well worth exploring at the start of this book.

As preparation for a discussion of the verbal propaganda that tends to keep hikers shod, I shall here present, more or less without comment, a comprehensive parade of the images associated with bare feet. I am referring here to the common symbolism of modern Western culture, as recognized and consciously employed by writers, artists, photographers, and advertisers working within and appealing to that culture.

While reviewing this parade, I invite the reader to judge the validity of the following contention: that most of our feelings—both pleasant and unpleasant—about bare feet are related to our sense of ever increasing separation from the rest of creation. Our ancestors may have gone barefoot as happily as the bears in the woods, but we are "civilized" now. So like it or not—we must wear shoes—especially in the woods, if for no other reason than to let the bears know who their betters are.

Images of Bare Feet

Bare feet are seen, in various situations as being:

carefree	dangerous
clean	disgraceful
comfortable	disrespectful
considerate	embarrassing
expressive	impolite
fun	improper
graceful	inconsiderate
healthy	irresponsible
human	shameful
impulsive	slovenly
natural	uncivilized
practical	uncomfortable
sensitive	unconventional
sensuous	unsanitary
uninhibited	vulnerable

Bare feet are seen, in various situations as showing:

confidence	backwardness
freedom	carelessness
independence	hopelessness
innocence	humility
simplicity	poverty
youth	unpreparedness

that one feels at ease
that one feels at home
that one feels at peace

An Exercise

Try studying a few advertising photographs wherein the choice has been made to present the model in bare feet, and ask yourself what images you think the photographer wanted the model's bare feet to evoke in each case.

CHAPTER II

What We Are Told About Bare Feet

Media Misconceptions

"....humans have soft feet and need shoes to protect them." Thus ended a short series of crude caricatures on comparative anatomy, included in a children's television program. I only took notice of this because I had the television on to amuse my children on a Saturday morning in the hours before taking them with me on a barefoot hike, and in that context it seemed rather ironic. I did not suppose, however, that this was any sort of propaganda attempt on the part of the shoe industry. At most, I supposed it to be an attempt to teach taxonomical concepts to build language skills in preschool children: cows have hooves, dogs have paws, humans have shoes, and so on. I was keenly aware of an underlying message that was here being repeated and reinforced (probably without any conscious thought) to wit: that we alone

5

among God's creatures, need shoes to protect our uniquely inadequate feet from a world naturally hostile to them.

The Interests of an Industry

Beyond this general idea that shoes are a necessity for humans, there is a further notion that they are especially essential to hikers, who require much heavier footwear to protect them from the hazards of the trail than they would need for street wear. This is largely—perhaps primarily—a reflection of the fact that heavy, cumbersome hiking boots are the principal product which can be sold to participants in what would otherwise be an uniquely inexpensive activity. It is most definitely in the interest of the manufacturers of athletic footwear in general, and hiking boots in particular, to reinforce the idea that human feet are poorly designed, and prone to painful failure under the stress of virtually any physical activity without the help of the very latest (and most expensive) in technically advanced footwear.

Although, as a businessman, I can well understand their natural interest in promoting such ideas, I feel none the less compelled to do all that I can to dispel them. It is simply a heartfelt sense of thankfulness for the more than twenty years of clean, healthy, and very rewarding pleasure that I have had from hiking barefoot that so compels me. Having such extensive experience not only as a barefoot hiker, but also as an instructor in barefoot hiking, I can quite honestly, and I hope quite credibly, reassure my readers.

There Is Nothing Uniquely Inadequate About Human Feet

Except in the coldest weather, when our circulatory systems are at a disadvantage in having to warm toes so far from our torsos, we can go barefoot as comfortably and as safely as cats and dogs. This is not to deny that there are some individuals with specific medical problems which necessitate that they take extraordinary measures to protect their feet from things that would otherwise pose no significant hazards. This unfortunate group, which includes diabetics and others with circulatory or dermatological problems placing their extremities at extreme risk of morbid infection, must, sadly, be enjoined against ever going barefoot. To extend such an harsh injunction, however, to healthy individuals would be to needlessly—and in my view unconscionably—deny them not only the use of one of their God-given senses, but a very special sense of creaturely freedom and a oneness with the rest of creation.

One of the saddest results of the all too effective propaganda in favor of footwear for the forest bound is that there are a substantial number of people who genuinely love going barefoot and do so almost everywhere, but who have nonetheless been convinced that they could never dare go barefoot in the woods. The truth is that forest trails are actually much easier on bare feet than paved streets, and generally safer than public beaches, and anyone who has ever gone barefoot in a forest will tell you that there is no nicer nor better place for going barefoot.

As for the rock scrambling that makes up such a favorite part of many good hikes, it need only be observed that a good many technical climbers rely on their bare feet as well as their bare hands to give them the sensitivity and the hold that they need on rock surfaces. All this is not to say that hiking trails present no hazards to bare feet, but that the hazards they present are easily overcome by cautious barefoot hikers who choose their footfalls and learn to depend on the well trained sensitivity of their bare soles as an added defense that renders them, if anything, less prone to injury than their shod companions. This sensitivity is nature's way of protecting the feet. By wearing shoes at all, shod hikers lose this valuable sensitivity, and also often fall into a dangerous carelessness about where they put their feet, which in turn necessitates shoes which are even heavier and more cumbersome to give them compensatory protection.

Bare feet have tough, flexible soles and strong, nimble toes designed not only to form themselves to the earth and often literally take hold of the roots and rocks and other irregularities of the trail (in a way which often makes the barefoot hiker seem—to the shod—to be phenomenally sure footed), but also act as a highly sophisticated sensory system adding immeasurably to the pleasure of hiking, as well as helping to ensure safety. Things are much different for shod hikers, whose feet only pay a price for the pleasures of their more privileged senses in corns, calluses, bunions, blisters, and "hot spots." Poor, sweating, malodorous, and often malformed appendages that they become, they tend to be regarded simply as a nuisance. They may be pampered to stop them from hurting, but no respect is given to them nor pleasure taken in them. Nonetheless, no matter how long mistreated in this way, they will, in most cases, after only a few short miles of being left unshod on forest trails, re-assert themselves to the point that it will soon again be apparent what pride and pleasure Providence must have taken in creating them.

CHAPTER III

An Historical Discussion

"Put off thy shoes from off thy feet,
    for the place whereon thou standest
    is holy ground."

—Exodus 3:5

Here we find one of the oldest, and perhaps best known references to shoes. As a former divinity student, I am well aware of the critical difficulties that might await me were I to presume to comment on such a text in detail; but I think it safe to assume at least the following:

1. The people for whose benefit these words were first written down must have been *acquainted* with shoes, even if the majority of them may actually have gone barefoot.

2. Shoes must have held some associations for them beyond the purely prosaic and practical.

Although a cursory inspection of a concordance will demonstrate that by the end of the Old Testament period these associations had become manifold and complex; a good many scholars might agree that one of the more important notions here is that the primary purpose of shoes is to insulate the wearer from casual contact with things on the ground that are regarded as unclean; and that therefore the shoes themselves are manifestly unclean. Although the Arabs have a similar notion, this is hardly surprising when one considers the historical, cultural, and religious parallels which can be drawn between the two nations, and in fact such ideas are very culture specific. This did not become part of the mental furniture of the Christian West because the early Christians quite deliberately rejected the Old Testament categories of clean and unclean.

Egyptians

Many of the most highly civilized of the ancient peoples seem to have made little if any use of any sort of footwear. The Egyptians left evidence of a limited use of ornamental footwear—such as the sort of soleless sandals actually referred to as "Cleopatras" in one of their twentieth century reincarnations—but virtually nothing that might have provided their soles with any practical covering.

Hindus

The Hindus, both at the height of their civilization and down through the many centuries to our own time, have perhaps been most like the Ancient Egyptians in making more use of ornamental than of functional footwear, but have been hardly alone, historically, among Aryan peoples in their more typical preference for simply going barefoot.

Greeks

The Greeks, from their Bronze Age beginnings until their absorption into the Roman Empire were certainly acquainted with shoes, but most of them—quite regardless of circumstances—preferred to go barefoot. Their soldiers, athletes, and philosophers—and most classical Greeks saw themselves as a bit of each—tended to regard footwear as decadent, unæsthetic, and somehow a violation of the Olympic ideal. Shoes among the Greeks were associated primarily with the theater, and with dandies, who like actors, wore them primarily as a means of increasing their stature. Gods and heroes are always shown barefooted in Greek art, and the typical Greek warrior, or hoplite, while depicted in body armor that includes heavy leg greaves, wears no shoes whatever. If art is to be believed, the Trojan war was fought in bare feet, and Alexander the Great set off to conquer half the world with barefoot armies.

Romans

The Roman Legions, however, were most definitely shod, and although in many ways the Romans tended to imitate the Greeks once they had conquered them, they did not imitate the Greek habit of going barefoot. Roman dress—both military and civil—was a sign of Roman power, and it was thus acquired by those who aspired to Roman Citizenship. With the exception of slaves, paupers, rustics, and religious ascetics, the Roman world—even the very large Greek-speaking part of it—was a shod world. Footwear would thenceforth confer not only corns, blisters, and bunions, but also a sense of civilization, social arrival, and even association—however tenuous—with the ruling establishment.

Kelts

The reader might well object that so far all the examples drawn have been of peoples living in very warm—if not decidedly hot—climates. At this point, it is appropriate to consider the Kelts, a people who throughout most of their history took a well attested pride in their cultural preference for going barefoot, and whose dedication to this practice seemed, if anything, to increase with geographic latitude. Probably the first Aryan people to colonize western Europe, these hearty folk once dominated much of the continent. Although most of the Keltic tribes suffered the cultural consequences of conquest (first by the Romans and then by various Germanic peoples) a few pockets of Keltic culture did manage to survive into modern times without significant compromise; the best example being in the Scottish Highlands.

Before the disastrous rebellion of 1745, the quelling whereof brought about the virtual end of their traditional culture, the great majority of the Keltic speaking (or even Keltic identifying) population went barefoot, and in many cases, did so the year round. This was true of both sexes, all ages, and all social classes, and although one might argue that the poor did so out of necessity, the wealthier classes, including the nobility, insisted on going barefoot not only because they found it comfortable to do so but also out of a sense of national pride. Their "Sassenach" neighbors to the South might have been so poorly endowed by nature as to have need of shoes, but they themselves found no use for them.

After the rebellion, Parliament passed a number of measures to ensure the rapid disappearance of any distinguishable Highland culture. Among these was the prohibition of Highland dress. Scottish settlers in the American Colonies were not affected by this and managed to retain Highland dress and the practice of going barefoot until at least the end of the 18th Century. Eventually, however, the relentless forces of assimilation ran faster even than the King's writ, and in the end this once proud culture all but disappeared from both the old world and the new, to survive only in the sad shadow world of "fancy-dress," where—to add insult to injury—all the "Highlanders" are quite daintily shod.

It should be noted that the costume of the fancy-dress Highlander derives primarily from the uniforms of Highland regiments which were later established within the British Army as a means of redirecting Scottish nationalism to serve the interests of the crown. These uniforms were designed to include not only shoes but a very distinctive and standardized form of socks. Most family tartans—especially those of more recent origin—tend to be illustrated in this regimental style, rather than in any pre-Hanoverian style.

Fashions and Customs

Bare feet have always been more prevalent when they have enjoyed the contextual support of a distinct local (or temporal) fashion. A good example of this can be found during the French Empire period, when a Grecian revival in the world of fashion encouraged a good many ladies, who might previously have been aghast at the idea, to make it their custom to go barefoot.

The tide of cultural assimilation, although generally favoring the shod, has also had some noteworthy counter currents, particularly the Irish, whose nationalism had never had such a strong sartorial element, but who were quite as fond of going barefoot as any of their fellow Kelts. Within a single generation, the English gentry who had been settled in Ireland by Henry VIII had "gone native" to the extent that in Elizabethan portraits they are typically shown elegantly attired and yet nonetheless barefooted. A similar development, albeit in a different social context, manifested itself in Victorian England, when Irish immigrants were blamed for spreading their custom of going barefoot among natives of the Liverpool area.

Barefoot to School

A number of years ago, while working among elderly patients at West London Hospital, I met a number of women who had grown up in various parts of Ireland around the turn of the century. Of those who had been educated—and most had—almost all said that they had gone barefoot to school and would never have thought of going shod. This had not been the result of poverty, lack of discipline, nor any negligent "come if you care to and wear what you like" policy on the part of educators. There had, I was told, often been strict discipline with regard to school uniforms. Bare feet had simply been the accepted, expected, and in some cases, even the required norm. What was wanted was a uniform, disciplined, conservative appearance that

would be pleasing and respectable but not osten-
tatious by community standards. That meant bare
feet.

During the same period, it was also quite common
for children in the rural areas of North America to go
barefoot to school. Here, however, the custom has
always been associated with rustic informality. There
may be a certain distant nostalgia for country ways,
but they are also seen as substandard—even by country folk. This is perhaps the reason that the number
of places permitting this particular practice has de-
creased so rapidly during our own century that any
present day survivals are quite rare. It seems typically
to have been suppressed as small, one-room school
houses were closed and the children who had once
walked barefoot to them began riding buses to larger
regional establishments upon whose newly polished
floors bare feet were deemed unwelcome.

There seem to have been a few stumbles in this
well-shod march to progress when school dress codes
came under attack in the early seventies. I once spoke
to a young woman who claimed that she often went
barefoot to just such a modern regional high school in
the mid-seventies and was not alone in doing so, but
such exceptions only prove what has since become an
increasingly firm rule.

Phantom Laws

Bare feet, in fact, have become unwelcome in an
increasing number of settings over the past half century. This has been especially true of eating establishments, but of late has extended to various other sorts

of shops. Although hardly fair when one considers how unlikely the unshod are to be careless about where they step, there is often an implication that bare feet are somehow unsanitary—especially when the signs enjoining against them attempt to attribute the proprietor's personal prejudices to some "Department of Health."

When I began this book, I thought it appropriate to research the history of such "regulations" and sent a letter of inquiry to the Waterbury Health Department. A few days later, I received a telephone call from Waterbury's Chief Sanitarian, Mr. Michael Carey, who informed me that he had checked with colleagues at the Connecticut Department of Health Services in Hartford, and that there existed *"no statutory basis"* for any regulations regarding footwear and that such requirements on the part of restaurants and shops were purely a matter of private policy.

Another mean little phantom law that often haunts the would-be barefooted is the supposed prohibition of barefoot driving. Here again, a careful search finds *no such statute in the state of Connecticut.* Such phantom laws may derive from actual laws in other jurisdictions. I regret, however, that I cannot do more than report the situation in Connecticut as a single (though I suspect not untypical) example, and suggest that interested readers inquire into the laws of their own localities. It may be that phantom laws are rather easily "enacted" by private citizens willing to "legislate" their private prejudices through rumor-mongering and wishful thinking. It is, nonetheless, difficult to imagine why bare feet should be the subject of such phantom legislation.

Third World Peoples

Until well past the middle of the twentieth century, most of the world's people went barefoot all their lives, just as their ancestors had always done. This was not, as seen in the case of the Kelts, only a warm climate phenomenon. The mountain people of the Andes, descendants of the once-proud Inca, always went barefoot, as did the Himalayan Sherpas half a world away. When Sir Edmund Hillary made the first conquest of Mt. Everest in 1953, his Sherpa bearers were almost all barefooted, even well above the snow line. Photographs from expeditions that followed in those brave footsteps only thirty years later, however, show all the Sherpas shod.

These same decades have seen tremendous changes everywhere, but particularly among the vast multitudes who have all but abandoned the incredibly rich cultural diversity of their ancestors to lose themselves in that T-shirted and plastic shod parody of Western Europe now known as the "Third World." This deplorable aping was perhaps inevitable, and once it had begun, it was no less inevitable that those who honored their former colonial masters with this sincerest form of flattery should find themselves referred to as "nations new to shoes" and react by wholeheartedly accepting—often as a matter of national social policy—the idea that barefootedness was a sign of backwardness.

Nudists

Real Europeans can, of course, be equally indecorous, especially those who have come of late to delight in appearing in exotic locations wearing *only* shoes. Perhaps this is intended to accentuate the fact that they are otherwise naked, or perhaps it is because these so-called "naturalists" are not quite prepared for an experience so natural as being in actual contact with the Earth, or again perhaps it is because they have managed to make of the feet that God gave them something considerably more shameful than any of the parts of themselves that they delight in exposing.

Franciscans

How different the examples of St. Francis and St. Clair, who taught their followers to modestly cover their bodies with the simplest of habits but to leave their feet completely bare. Going barefoot was for them primarily an expression of the idea of religious poverty. The vow of poverty—which St. Francis redefined as something much more rigorous than it had been in the old monastic world—was not so much a commitment to solidarity with the poor (although that idea was certainly included within it) as a commitment to place oneself in a position of total dependence upon God's providence rather than one's own or any other human providence [cf. Mat. 10:10.]. Bare feet were God-given and thus sufficient unto themselves. Related to the idea of religious poverty were ideas of discipline, humility, and self-denial, which bare feet also symbolized. These remarkable saints and their first followers would, moreover, have had another very joyful and deeply spiritual reason for going barefoot. St. Francis, famous as he still is for preaching to the birds, expressed in many ways a deep reverence for the whole of creation as the Creator's handiwork, and it is quite probable that he would have seen the injunction of Exodus 3:5 as applying to the whole of God's Earth.

CHAPTER IV

Of Environmental Interest

A major theme—perhaps the dominant theme—in the first three chapters of this book has been the steady growth, throughout the history of our civilization, of the idea that all the rest of creation greets us with a peculiar hostility unknown to any other creatures; that Nature is at constant war with us, and that we dare not tread her vales unshod. A counter theme, however, has also been presented: that there have always been those who have rejected this notion, seeing it perhaps as a projection of our own guilt over the oft suppressed but ever haunting knowledge that *we*, in fact, are the aggressors; and that many who have joined this often small but seldom silent counter-chorus have, as a sign of their own peace and friendship with the Earth, chosen to go barefoot. Counting myself among these last, I shall, in this chapter, try to show some sound reasons—both real and symbolic—why today's environmentalists should seriously consider committing themselves to the same choice.

The most solid and tangible argument favoring bare feet from the environmental point of view concerns the impact of trail users on the trails themselves, and the unfortunate necessity faced by those who maintain the trails of shifting them from time to time to reduce what can, in some places, be a serious erosion problem. Walking barefoot, as Nature intended, humans hardly disturb even the most delicate ground cover, and can delight in the soft, carpet-like, feel of moss in good conscience. Shoes, however, can be very damaging to even the most resilient grass cover. Hard and unyielding, they do not gently mold themselves to the earth as bare soles do, but rather stamp into her the rude signature of their treads. Shoes leave a mark on even the firmest ground, while bare feet hardly print in the softest. Thus a whole troop of barefoot hikers will cause less trail damage than a single hiker in shoes.

Bare feet are also silent, often barely whispering to the ground, even when running; and even when heard, making a sound which seems much more to belong in the forest than the sound of shoes.

Beyond these there are symbolic and spiritual reasons for hiking barefoot which should be just as important to those who profess a love and respect for the Earth and for those of their fellow creatures who must make their homes in the environments which they, as hikers, visit. Going barefoot allows the hiker a deeper, more respectful, and much more rewarding relationship with Nature. I have known at least one woman who made a very deliberate and thoughtful decision to go barefoot entirely out of concern for the impact she was having on forest trails, and was subsequently delighted that Nature should have rewarded her not only with the sense of "safe conduct" which her trust had anticipated, but also with a tremendous increase in the pleasure she could derive from hiking now that the soles of her feet were bare and able to feel the Earth under them.

One could hardly imagine a barefoot hiker littering, and in fact, the unshod quickly develop an instinct for removing from a trail such things as do not belong there. They take both pride and pleasure in knowing that their bare feet are trail-friendly; and they tend to extend this pride and pleasure to doing what they can to keep the trails foot-friendly, not only for the fellow humans whom they hope might follow them in going barefoot, but for all the many wonderful kinds of warm bare feet that by God's grace walk the Earth.

CHAPTER V

Getting Back to Going Barefoot: Six More Misconceptions

In my twenty-odd years of barefoot hiking I have encountered each of the following misconceptions many times and would like now to put them to rest.

"Bare Feet Need Many Months of Conditioning"

The initial time and effort needed to condition bare feet for hiking is very much less than anyone who has not had experience in the area would tend to suppose. Two or three miles of walking barefoot on good forest trails, two or three times a week, for two or three weeks will prepare almost any hiker to set off quite confidently barefooted on almost any hike that might be included in the program of any hiking group, provided only that the weather be relatively mild.

Although the general strengthening of the ligaments under the soles of the feet is a very important part of this process, the actual thickening of the soles themselves (contrary to a related misconception which is also in part the subject of the next paragraph) is actually the *least* important part of the conditioning process. The sole thickens very quickly—within days, in fact—when stimulated by highly textured surfaces, but it also wears down quickly when exposed to abrasive surfaces such as pavement. Chapter 9 describes the practice of running barefoot on gravel as a way of toughening soles, but this unusual expedient is of only short term value. Forest walking quickly and very pleasurably develops and maintains soles quite thick enough for any weekend hiking.

"Bare Feet Become Callused, Bruised, Torn, and Stained"

Most of the surfaces encountered in hiking do not soil or stain bare feet, but rather tend to cleanse them to the point that they are quite pleasant to the touch when felt and examined. As you learn to hike barefoot, you should develop the habit of examining your bare feet often and comparing them by touch to those of others who go barefoot. You will not only find a good deal of variation among the soles of different people, but also a surprising variation in the texture of your own soles, both at different times of the year and at different times of the day. Most of this is due to the tension of underlying muscles and tendons, and the quality of the sole itself takes practice to assess. You should not find any calluses on the soles of a barefoot hiker. Calluses on the soles generally come from wearing hard, poorly fitted shoes—not from going barefoot. They are no advantage to the barefoot hiker and should be worn off by walking on pavement or sand, or—when they occur in areas that cannot benefit from such natural abrasion, such as the margins of the heels, reduced with pumice or very coarse sand paper. If left, they will tend to crack when subjected to the otherwise healthy flexing of the soles during barefoot hiking. Such cracks are very painful and difficult to heal once they have formed. For this same reason, a barefoot hiker's soles should always be kept moist and supple with lotion or lanolin, as dry soles also tend to crack—especially in cold weather. Cuts and bruises should be rare, as these are a sign of careless walking habits that a barefoot hiker should be very concerned about.

"Bare Feet Become Insensitive to Everything"

The truth is that any slight reduction in potential sensitivity resulting from the thickening of parts of our soles is far outweighed by the continual development and refinement, through use, of the entire sensory system. This includes not only a phenomenal number of various sorts of sensory receptors situated in our soles, but also very significant portions of our brains which Nature has reserved to the purpose of corresponding with them. Our soles may, like our palms, be quite properly regarded as specialized organs of our sense of touch, and it is hardly an exaggeration to say that they are capable of developing a sensitivity so keen that they can almost *taste* the richness of the earth underneath them. This sensitivity, however, as we shall see in the next section, can only be developed by walking barefoot over as wide a variety of surfaces as possible.

"One Must Learn to Mentally Block Out All Sensation"

This alternative conclusion, different as it seems from the previous, derives from the same mistaken observations, and is not only equally incorrect, but far more counterproductive.

There *is* an important element of mental conditioning involved in learning to hike in bare feet, but it has nothing to do with "mind over matter," nor with any denial either of physical reality or of our own senses. Our mental conditioning aims rather at the full development of that marvelous sensory system described above, in a way intended to overcome whatever atrophy it may have suffered through being denied, thwarted, and distorted by the habit of wearing shoes. If you will permit an analogy, imagine a man who has lived all of his life in a society which, perhaps because of hazardous noise in its history, had provided everyone from earliest childhood with thick earmuffs and abandoned speech as a means of communication. One day our hypothetical friend travels outside the boundaries of his own society and encounters people who do not wear earmuffs and convince him at length by dumb mime to uncover his ears. He does not at first hear anything like what they hear, but only a rush of very uncomfortable noise. Only with time do the various sounds begin to sort themselves out in his mind, and although he begins within the hour to take a real pleasure in listening, it is months before he can cope with the subtleties of speech well enough to begin to learn a language. Such is the case when one begins to hike barefoot. At first, the unfamiliar

textures overwhelm the tactile senses. The mind, unprepared and unaccustomed to any sensation from the
soles beyond that of the even rise and fall of the body's
own weight, automatically reacts with alarm and may
even label them as painful. As the sensations sort
themselves out, however, the hiker becomes comfortable with them. Although the full process of attuning
and mentally calibrating these tactile senses (until
the soles, like the palms, at last come into their own
as specialized sense organs) takes many months, a
very substantial beginning can be made in only a few
minutes, and the learning process itself thereafter becomes quite pleasant. A few minutes of conscious
mental preconditioning before beginning the actual
walk can be very helpful here. If the power of the will
is used not to banish but to *welcome* the new sensations, the whole process will take far less time than it
otherwise would and be far more pleasant.

(A very exceptional case, which may be attributed
to an extraordinary aptitude for such mental preconditioning, is reported in the final chapter of this book,
in the section, "Shoeless in the Forest".)

One other phenomenon, which most will probably experience for themselves, should also be mentioned here. Even an experienced barefoot hiker will
notice when crossing a gravel road at the very start
of a hike a slight echo of that sense of alarm felt
by the first-time barefoot hiker under similar circumstances. The experienced barefoot hiker manages to
adjust and attune his senses very quickly, however, to
the extent that crossing a virtually identical gravel
road even a few minutes into the hike produces no
such sensation: unless, that is, he very deliberately
concentrates—as I often do when leading first-time

barefoot hikers—on feeling the gravel as a first-timer would feel it.

"One Must Go Barefoot Constantly to Stay in Condition"

One does *not* need to go barefoot constantly, or even regularly, to retain the ability to do so comfortably. This is because the short term thickening of the soles through stimulation is relatively minor and unimportant. Much more important is the process of learning to use the soles' exquisite sense of touch, and this is more or less permanent. It all comes back almost instantly, even after months of being shod. I learned this for myself having recently spent a period of nine or ten months during which, because of unusual demands on my time, I was unable to hike, and hardly able at all to go barefoot. At the end of this time, when the opportunity again presented itself, I set off barefoot, with no preparation whatever, on a ten mile hike which I enjoyed immensely. That evening, my feet felt somewhat sore, but only with the same deep muscle soreness that I felt in my legs as a result of so long a walk after such relative idleness. My soles were clean, unbruised, and unmarked and felt much healthier for the walk. A regular schedule of hiking, although much to be recommended from a general health point of view, is not actually necessary to maintain the condition of bare feet for ordinary forest hiking. Once you have started hiking barefoot, it is a very good idea to do *all* your hiking in bare feet and save your shoes for manmade surfaces only. This is to avoid falling back into inappropriate hiking habits which could be dangerous. The rule to keep is: "Bare ground? *Bare feet!*"

"Wearing Shoes Will Become Very Uncomfortable"

It is probable that once you have grown accustomed to going barefoot, you will have less liking for shoes and find it more of a blessing to get them off after a day spent wearing them—especially if it were a hot day. You are also likely to be much less tolerant of shoes that do not fit well. So much the better. On the other hand, you should have no problem wearing sensible, properly fitted shoes in comfortable weather.

I can say from my own experience that during the years that I spent more or less living in London, I would frequently spend the whole of one day rambling barefoot through the countryside and the whole of the next walking along city pavements in ordinary dress shoes without the least discomfort in either case. I would tend in fact to think that my feet were in better condition—even for shod pavement walking—for all the miles of barefoot hiking that I had done.

CHAPTER VI

Biological Hazards

Need for Specific Local Advice

Many people who might otherwise enjoy barefoot hiking are deterred by quite irrational fears concerning such things as might be subsumed under the category of "Biological Hazards". This is not to say that there are not legitimate concerns in this area and reasons to exercise caution. All hikers—barefoot or shod—should be aware of such poisonous, parasitic, or otherwise harmful animals and plants as may be encountered in the part of the world where they are hiking so that they can watch for and avoid them. In fact, this applies not only to hikers, but, like being immunized against tetanus every ten years, is to be recommended to anyone engaged in any outdoor activity.

I can say of Connecticut, where I now make my home, that poison ivy is perhaps the principal such hazard, as venomous creatures, other than hornets and their kin, are extremely rare and seldom encountered. I would not venture to say over what portions of North America the same might be true, but I am aware that in some areas the situation is very different.

General Precautions

In any case, barefoot hikers should be maintaining a level of cautious attention that more than compensates for their slightly increased exposure. Remember to step up onto a fallen log or other low obstruction before you step over it and generally avoid placing your hands or feet anywhere that you have not yet been able to survey with your eyes.

Barefoot hikers do need a bit more insect repellent than the shod, and have a bit more of themselves to check for ticks and other parasites when conditions so indicate. As a defense against ticks, repellent should be applied not only to bare feet, but also to legs well up under their trousers, and to arms well up under their sleeves, as well as to neck and shoulder areas under the collar, since these pests like to migrate from exposed extremities toward the warmer, covered parts of the body. Some recommend that the trousers themselves be treated with insecticide and left to dry before wearing; but one must be careful, as the end result of this might in itself be irritating and perhaps even hazardous to the skin.

Climates characterized by frequent freezing of the ground during winter tend to spare their inhabitants from most of the more unpleasant creepy-crawlies. As to such microscopic parasites that may attack humans through their feet, these are generally associated either with the presence of human excrement, or with very intense human traffic, and these hazards also are of much greater concern in warmer climates.

At the end of the day, it is a matter of personal philosophy whether we live in fear of the natural environment as something alien and hostile to us, or consider ourselves at home in it and as well equipped by Nature to deal with it as are any of her creatures.

CHAPTER VII

Spring: A Barefoot Beginning

Ideal Conditions Not to Wait For

The best time to begin barefoot hiking is in the early spring, when the days are beginning to grow warm, and frost has become so infrequent a visitor that the ground holds no trace of it, even at night. This is the natural time for beginnings, when the earth brings forth new life and invites her creatures to new experiences. The streams run full and invite the unshod to wade through their cool, life-giving waters. The snows of winter have come and gone, leaving the leaves of autumn pressed into a mulch now well on the way to weathering into yet another layer of soil so rich bare soles can almost taste it. Here and there, young plants break through the forest floor, harbingers of the lush growth that may in months to come obscure it, but the first-time barefoot hiker can still see its surface easily now, and thus can walk in greater confidence. Sometimes in that special season, just as spring arrives, she may grant bare feet the special pleasure of a patch of cool, clean snow melting in the warm sun—tarrying a moment for toes to touch and test it before it disappears. Finally, it should be said that feet going bare for the first time in spring will have many months to condition themselves before facing their first frosty morning in mid-autumn.

Genuine as these advantages are, they are *not* reason enough to recommend that an interested reader who might pick up this book in the late summer or early autumn wait six or eight months before enjoying the experience of barefoot hiking. I both hike barefoot myself and lead barefoot hikes the year round, and I have taken first-time barefoot hikers onto the trails of Western Connecticut at virtually all times of the year (when the weather has been reasonable) with equal degrees of delight and pleasure on their part. I *do* recommend that your first barefoot experience be on a mild, dry, sunny day; but that day might well fall in February. Just take the first good day that comes along.

Woodland trails are best for the first-time barefoot hiker. They are generally very easy on bare soles and reward them with a great deal of pleasure—but again, this is not a must. A walk through fields and meadows can also be pleasant; and I have one good friend who chose a fairly challenging rock scramble as her first barefoot experience. If you have a choice, a walk through woods is both the most pleasurable experience for bare feet—especially feet going bare for the first time—and the best learning experience for them.

Gaining Confidence

Furthermore, it is best—though, again, not at all necessary—that on your first barefoot hike you place your bare feet firmly in the hands, as it were, of someone who always hikes barefoot and has been hiking barefoot for some time.

An experienced barefoot hiker who has any ability as an instructor will not only help you to learn about your bare feet, and how to care for them, enjoy them, and use them safely, but will also help you develop a real confidence and pride in them far more quickly than you might on your own. When it comes to learning to absolutely *rely* on your bare feet, there is nothing more helpful than the example of a good teacher.

If you cannot find such a teacher, then a barefoot companion who has done at least *some* barefoot hiking would be the next best alternative, and even the company of another person who is going barefoot for the first time would be helpful. If you cannot find anyone else to share your first barefoot experience, then go alone and take this book as your companion. It has been written with the intention of serving you in just that way if need be.

Once you have full confidence in your bare feet, and the sense of pride that is quite appropriate to that confidence when it is based upon sound experience, you will be quite happy to go along as the only barefoot hiker in an otherwise shod group just for the fun of seeing how many converts you might be able to make. It will not take you all that long to develop that confidence, but until you have it, you should not even consider putting yourself in such a position. The test to apply to yourself is this: Until or unless you have enough confidence in your bare feet simply to leave your shoes at home, you should not risk what little confidence you may have in a situation wherein even the most friendly questions from your companions might make you feel doubtful, self-conscious, and un-comfortable. Most of us, as mentioned in previous chapters, have been burdened with subconscious fears about going barefoot, and overcoming them gen-erally requires some conscious and deliberate psycho-logical self-preparation. The advice in this chapter which deals with such preparation is often quite as important as the purely practical advice to be found alongside it.

Before moving on completely from this discussion of the inadvisability of hiking barefoot for the first time with a shod group, an important exception should be noted: If you find that at least one other person intends to go barefoot—especially if you learn that that person is an experienced barefoot hiker—then you have found a very good situation for your own first barefoot experience. You should by all means take the opportunity, for even in this type of circumstance, walking barefoot will definitely build your confidence. I have taught several people to go barefoot under just such circumstances, people who just decided on the spot to take off their shoes on my example. Your own example will soon be just as persuasive.

Let us assume for the present, however, that you have chosen to enjoy your first barefoot experience in complete solitude. Unless you are exceptionally for-tunate, you will probably not be able to arrange for yourself all, or even most, of the ideal circumstances recommended here. Do what you can to make that experience as perfect as possible, but do not make the mistake of putting it off to wait for the perfect day. If that perfect day comes for you—as it probably will—after you are already an experienced barefoot hiker, it will be just as perfect and probably more so. Afford yourself whatever time you can for *now*, and enjoy it.

Leaving Shoes at Home

If at all possible, and you can find the confidence to do so, I would strongly recommend that you leave your shoes at home when you set off on your first barefoot hike. This is important both to build your confidence and to set your mood. Try as well, if you can possibly get away with it, to go barefoot throughout the entire day from morning to night. When you finish your walk your feet will be highly sensitized and then should be left bare to enjoy this sensitivity. You will want to do this every time you hike, although it may not always be practical, but you should make a special effort to honor the day of your first barefoot hike in this way.

Advantages of a Nature Center

With the bare, trail-wise feet of an experienced teacher to mark the way for your own, you will not have to worry so much where you go. Setting out alone, however, or with another first-time barefoot hiker, you will do well to seek out the safety of the somewhat controlled environment of a well maintained nature center or wildlife sanctuary, not only for your first, but perhaps your first half dozen shoeless excursions. Unlike state parks and municipal recreation facilities, they do not seem to attract youthful drinkers, casual picnickers, nor others who are given to littering. Their trails tend to be well cared for, and because they are typically set out with the intent of providing visitors with access to a number of mini-environments, they provide bare feet with the opportunity to sample a surprising variety of surfaces. Most of these centers are maintained by small trust foundations, although larger organizations such as the National Audubon Society, are also responsible for a great many of them. Unlike state parks, they tend not to appear on small maps, but most of them do have telephone listings and they are actually more numerous than you might imagine.

When you arrive at one of these wonderful places, you will usually find a small office or "trail house" with a few nature exhibits and an attendant. She may be a part-time volunteer or perhaps a research student who more or less lives there. Ask her about the trails and tell her that you are going barefoot. You may well find that she is barefooted herself, and full of encouragement and advice for you. At the very least, she will be able to provide you with a trail map, for which there will probably be no charge. If the center is fairly close to your home, you will want to visit it frequently, even after you have graduated to more ambitious trails. Do what you can to support it. Get to know all of the staff well, and by all means, bring some friends.

Spend as much time on the trails as you can, but do not set any goals for yourself with regard to distance. You should have only one objective on this first day: to learn to go barefoot *safely*.

Stepping Straight Down

The first and most important safety rule is ALWAYS STEP *STRAIGHT DOWN!* NEVER ALLOW YOUR BARE FEET TO KICK, SHUFFLE, OR DRAG ALONG

THE GROUND. You must practice this rule faithfully. It is more important than all of the other rules taken together. It is more important than everything else you will read in this book. It is the very first thing to be said to any first-time barefoot hiker. This may require some conscious effort at first. You may well find that you have some bad walking habits to unlearn. Please note that this does *not* imply anything like stomping or stamping. The tread of the barefoot hiker is light, soft, and sensitive, often it is wary and tentative, but it is always deliberate and it is always *straight down*. If you learn to follow this one rule, even if you learn nothing else, you will already have eliminated at least 99 percent of the risk that any trail might pose to your bare feet.

The principle is well illustrated by the popular stage act wherein a performer—usually a small slight girl—walks up a ladder of swords in her bare feet. A cabbage is then sliced to slaw on the blades to prove that they are indeed razor sharp and someone from the audience is asked to come up and examine her bare soles. They prove to be deeply creased from her climb but there is no evidence of their having been actually cut. The audience assumes that she must have subjected her soles to some singularly Spartan regimen to bring them to a superhuman hardness. She probably *does* make a practice of going barefoot but the importance of this would be much more to strengthen and sensitize her feet than to toughen their soles. Although factors such as balance and weight distribution are also important, the key element in her technique is stepping straight down onto the blades and not allowing her soles to slide along them even to the slightest degree. Her act may also include walking across an area that has been completely covered with broken glass. Fearful as this seems to the wincing audience, all of whom have been warned about broken glass many times in their lives, as long as she steps properly, there is almost no risk at all that she will be cut. It is window glass to begin with, and it is all lying fairly flat. Broken glass, by the way, is a hazard to the barefoot hiker, but it is nowhere near the top of the list, and you will soon learn the precautions necessary to deal safely with it.

Watching the Path Ahead

The second safety rule for the barefoot hiker is ALWAYS WATCH THE PATH AHEAD. This may seem painfully obvious; but it can be painfully easy to forget. Always stop when you want to look at something off the path. Whenever your bare feet are in motion, your eyes must be in motion along with them, scanning the path up as far as it is visible and then back down to those bare feet. Their most frequent focus, however, should be on the part of the path two or three paces in front of your bare feet.

Learn to pick the spot for each footfall about this far in advance and try to anticipate what that particular piece of ground will feel like under foot when you get to it. This practice will become very important when you are hiking on stony or otherwise uneven terrain. You should definitely begin it on your first day of barefoot hiking even if you are on the mildest of trails. Being a matter of sensory coordination, much like catching a ball, it is a skill that develops mostly on an unconscious level, but you can consciously help it along by contemplating the fact that you are learning to coordinate two of your senses: the sight of your eyes and the newly discovered tactile sensitivity of your bare soles.

Keeping Weight Off Heels

Another habit which you should now begin consciously trying to form is that of keeping your weight on the balls of your feet, and not on your heels. This does *not* mean that you should constantly be walking up so high on your toes that your heels never touch the ground at all. Although there are circumstances—which I shall discuss later—where you will want to do just that. Such a gait would be both unnatural and unnecessary on ordinary trail surfaces, and would cause enormous fatigue in your calves within a very short time. What *is* meant is that you should try, within comfortable limits, to keep more of your weight on the forward part of the foot, and to keep it there for a longer time during the course of each step, than might previously have been your habit, and to put that much less weight on the heel.

To understand the reason for this you need only examine a typical pair of bare feet. Start with the heels. Even in the case of a person who has never gone barefoot you will usually notice that the skin covering them is very thick and hard. The total thickness may easily amount to a quarter of an inch, most of which is virtually dead callus. Between this apparently formidable part of the sole and the bone of the heel is a cushion of very tough and very resilient tissue. Yet as efficient a shock absorber as this cushion proves to be when one considers that it is no more than half an inch thick, it definitely has its limitations.

Nevertheless the apparent toughness of the heel, to-gether with its relative insensitivity when compared with the rest of the sole, would lead many of those who have no experience whatever of going barefoot to the false conclusion that if they had to go barefoot, they would do best to walk on their heels.

Moving on to the middle of the foot, you will find the cannon bones, or metatarsals. Although they form part of a shock absorption system that is far more effective than the simple cushion of the heel, they are themselves rather easily fractured. The hollow area on the inside of the sole where the metatarsal arch is at its highest is relatively tender and vulnerable, as this part of the sole usually does not touch the ground and thus rarely gets a chance to toughen, even in the case of someone who never wears shoes. The portion along the outside of the arch is usually fairly well toughened but a sharp impact here could nonetheless cause a metatarsal fracture.

Now probe and examine the ball of the foot. Supple and yielding, yet tough and resilient, this is both the most sensitive part of the sole and the part whereupon nature intended that most of the weight of the body should be borne. Notice how broad this part of the foot is and how much larger an area it presents to the ground than does the heel. Feel how flexible it is, how not only each of the toes, but each of the meta-tarsals behind the toes, can move up and down inde-pendently to mold to the contour of the earth. Feel the flexibility and strength of all the joints that allow the front part of the foot to absorb shock so much better than the heel.

Feel the strength and flexibility of the toes, which allow them not only to grip the earth and mold to it, but also to lift the trailing foot off the ground at the end of each step while propelling the body forward. Notice also that the pads of those toes are quite as sensitive as your fingers, and that the valley behind them is also especially sensitive to touch.

Finally, notice the overall quality of the padding of the ball of the foot. It is generally softer and more "giving" than that of the heel, but because this padding, unlike that of the heel, has muscular layers underlying it, the overall firmness of the ball of the foot can be varied, with practice, more or less at will.

It should be mentioned that while the foregoing paragraphs might simply be *read*, they might also be taken as a practice exercise. Borrowing the bare feet of a friend—particularly an habitually barefooted friend—would be a very valuable "hands on" experience, even if your friend has no hiking experience *per se*. This might be just the friend to talk into going along with you on your first visit to the sanctuary.

Getting back to the comparisons drawn between heels and toes, you should now be able to understand why keeping most of your weight on the balls of your feet will help the many joints that intervene between the arches and the toes to do their job of absorbing the shock of walking and saving you the pains in your shins and knees that come of landing too much of the force of each step on the heel.

You should also be able to understand why as a barefoot hiker you will be less prone to injury if you keep more of your weight on the balls of your feet, not only because they are much more yielding than your heels and therefore much less likely to be cut or bruised by sharp objects, but also because their greater sensitivity protects them.

Forming Habits of Awareness

Here we return again to the all-important subject of sensitivity and awareness. You must never forget that you are going barefoot, and you must always devote a part of your attention—your consciousness, if you will—to your bare soles. It was stated above that the tread of the barefoot hiker should always be soft and light, and that sometimes it must be wary and tentative. There are situations, some of which will come up later on in this book, when you will want to keep yourself wary enough to be prepared to retract a step if you do not like the feel of what you are stepping on. At such times, you may have to devote almost all of your attention to your bare soles, especially if you have not been going barefoot long enough to safely and confidently entrust this vigilance to the same subconscious portion of your mind that has always had responsibility for your feet. As with any skill that you might ever wish to acquire, you must ultimately commit the practical points of safe barefoot hiking to the realm of unconscious habits, but you must at first be willing to invest a substantial part of your conscious attention to the proper formation of those all important habits.

Walking with Eyes Closed

When you begin your first barefoot walk, you should walk very slowly. Feel your bare soles mold themselves to the ground with each step. If you have a friend with you, take turns at walking with your eyes closed and being guided by the hand. This is something that I always try to do with first-time barefoot hikers. While you have your eyes closed, try to shut out *everything* from your consciousness but your bare feet. Have your friend guide you in silence, and give no conscious thought to the hand holding yours. Nothing should exist for you but your bare feet and the bare ground underneath them. With just a bit more experience, you might even try walking by yourself with your eyes closed, and using the sensitivity of your bare feet to keep them on the trail, but you should only try this on a fairly smooth, level path, through an open, hazard free area, and only after you have previously walked over it with your eyes open to make sure that there are no hazards on the ground.

Experiencing Various Surfaces

Try to walk on, and get the feel of, as many different surfaces as you can find—earth, sand, grass, or moss—and do not avoid, except perhaps in the first hours, the more textured surfaces such as gravel; just take them in stride and notice what they actually feel like. Here you must discipline your mind not to interpret as painful anything which does not actually threaten to harm you. This discipline is absolutely essential to those who intend to rely on the sensitivity of their bare soles.

More Ambitious Hiking

Try to walk barefoot like this at least once a week (two or three times a week would be better), and generally try to go barefoot as much as possible. After walking a half dozen times in a sanctuary setting and covering a dozen or so miles, you can progress to deep forest trails. Try asking the staff at the center for advice on this. Someone there is sure to know something about trails in the local area, and they may even have books and maps available to help get you started. You will probably not find these trails all that much more demanding than those of the nature center, but you will almost certainly not find them maintained to the same standards. You will need to be more vigilant in watching for small, sharp stones imbedded in the trail and also for litter near road crossings. Watch also for the tiny stumps that remain where saplings have been cleared from the trail by cutting. You may encounter this unfortunate trail management practice even in the nature center, especially in areas where the staff has had to deal with fast spreading shrubs such as laurel, so be extra watchful when you see such shrubs along the trail. Even if it is not all that demanding, the typical terrain of a forest is generally not so tame as that of a nature center and you may have to do a bit of scrambling. This is generally much easier with bare feet than it would be shod, but you should still be careful, especially going downhill on soft earth. Take it slowly and dig into the earth with your toes as much as you can. Use the full surface of your soles to keep yourself from sliding. Choose your footfalls carefully as you scramble over rocks and tree roots. Use your toes. Always take the fullest advantage of the fact that your feet are bare. You will soon become very sure-footed.

Aching Calves

As your feet and legs adjust to barefoot hiking, you may experience certain sensations which, especially if very pronounced, might cause some concern in those unprepared for them. If you have never hiked barefoot before, and begin with a hike of more than two or three miles, especially with some considerable amount of downhill walking, you will probably experience an aching soreness in the soles of your feet and—even more likely—in the calves of your legs. This generally sets in after three or four hours and lasts only a day. It is the natural result of using and stretching muscles and tendons in your calves and soles in ways to which they are not accustomed. So long as these aches and pains are confined more or less to the evening following the hike, they are a very healthy sign of a good workout; and, if you hike again a few days later, it will probably take half again as much mileage to produce a similar sensation, so well will your feet and legs have been conditioned. If, however, you have discomfort in your feet which does not pass within a day or so, or any frank bruising, it is a sign that you took on a much more strenuous barefoot hike than you were ready for. You should not hike again until all discomfort passes and then begin again on a much easier trail or a section with only a fraction of the mileage attempted previously, and build up the distance gradually. If the discomfort can be seen as another chapter in a history of foot problems which you might have hoped, not unreasonably, that barefoot hiking might have solved, you should seek the advice of a physician, unless of course you have already been advised as to the nature of the problem, in which case—again—wait and start again at an easier level. While it is generally true of our bodies that use stretches capacity, too much, too soon, can mean far more pain than gain.

Itching Soles

Another phenomenon that you may experience from time to time is an itching sensation in the soles of your feet. This is caused by the rapid growth and thickening of the skin after stimulation. In most cases, walking barefoot on gravel will bring relief without stimulating any further skin growth once your soles have attained a good working thickness.

CHAPTER VIII

Summer:
Barefoot Almost Everywhere

Fully Conditioned Feet

If, as we have assumed, you began going barefoot some time in April, and have continued in this practice with a reasonable degree of regularity, you should, by the end of June, find your feet so thoroughly accustomed and conditioned to going bare, that you neither need nor want any shoes for any reason except, perhaps, to satisfy the dress code of some dining establishment, or—much more rarely—to deal with some very unusual (and almost always manmade) environmental hazard. Your bare soles are now reasonably well toughened, but more important is the fact that the muscles and tendons in your feet and legs have been stretched and strengthened to the point that you can now cope more comfortably with virtually any terrain in your bare feet than you could in shoes. Most important of all is the fact that you have learned the first lessons of sensitivity and awareness well enough to allow you to thoroughly enjoy going barefoot and to do so in perfect safety.

Finding a Hiking Group, or Founding One

Now that your bare feet are ready, you will want to expand your repertoire of trails and widen the variety of your hiking experience. One very effective and very enjoyable way to do this is to join a hiking group. If you cannot find one that is convenient for you in your area, you may want to consider founding a group of Barefoot Hikers. You will find advice on this subject in the final chapter of this book, but, as you will see there, I would not recommend that you consider taking on such a task until you yourself have had at least another full year of experience as a barefoot hiker. If founding such a group should, however, be your destiny, I would all the more urge you to get some experience of a good active hiking group now, even if it be a shod group and you have to travel some distance to join up with them. I would even more strongly recommend membership in a national organization, such as the Ramblers Association in the United Kingdom or the Sierra Club in the United States, to both of which I have myself belonged. You should, in fact, establish and maintain contacts with as many such organizations as possible, *especially* if you are considering founding one of your own.

As I explained in the previous chapter, now that you have a full confidence in your bare feet, you need not be concerned that you might well be the only barefoot hiker in an otherwise shod group. However, it is very important that you do all that you can, from the very onset, to make the leader and everyone else in the group as comfortable about your bare feet as you yourself are. Always remember that a good leader feels a genuine responsibility for the safety of everyone in the group and you will understand why it is both courteous and prudent for you to be positive, confident, and above all thoroughly open about the fact that you go barefoot. Virtually any group leader will welcome a responsible and well-prepared barefoot hiker, but it is up to *you* to give assurance that you are such. Always let the leader, and other hikers as well, feel and examine your bare soles. Shod and unshod companions alike tend to want to do this, although the shod are sometimes shy about it.

To put this in perspective, I should tell you that having, over the years, enjoyed the company of scores of leaders in dozens of different hiking groups, I have only once had any reservations expressed to me about my going barefoot. This was with the Appalachian Mountain Club, an organization wherein I must say— with approval—that the responsibilities of leadership are taken very seriously, and the leader, typical of this group, was an extremely conscientious young woman. She did not ask me to wear shoes but she did insist that I carry some with me. Halfway through the walk, she stopped to remove her boots and attend to blisters on her own feet, and when she then examined mine and found that they were free not only of blisters, but of any other sign of harm, she was rather apologetic.

What to Wear

Take pride in your bare feet, and take the very best care of them. In summer especially, you should keep to a strict rule of going barefoot whenever and wherever you can. With your bare feet thus braving the consequences of constant display, you will not want them to draw any negative attention to themselves. They should never appear soiled, bruised, or abused but as naturally and matter-of-factly bare as your hands. Try always to dress in such a way that your bare feet will appear to have been the most attractive and appropriate choice to complement your outfit. Be aware, however, that projecting a sense of this appropriateness depends much more on your state of mind than on your choice of clothing. Many who make it their custom to go barefoot virtually everywhere swear by soleless sandals, which often consist of little more than soft leather thongs, but which allow them to go attractively baresoled, if not entirely barefooted, almost anywhere, and which can be easily undone and discreetly returned to purses or pockets when no longer wanted.

What to Carry

As your hikes become longer and more diverse, and especially as you become involved in all-day social hiking, you will need to pay more attention to what you carry and how you carry it. In summer, the most important item is always *water*. On a very hot day, a hiker can easily require a pint of water every two hours. To conveniently carry an adequate supply, you should choose a sturdy, half-gallon plastic bottle with a tightly fitting screw-down cap. Remember that it will be jostled about and even turned upside down in your day pack and yet it *must not leak*. Unfortunately, since such a bottle will weigh four or five pounds when full, you must be careful both how you pack it and what you pack alongside it, being especially careful of any food you may be carrying.

Packing a soft, warm pullover is a good idea even in summer as it will both provide insurance against the possibility of a rapid fall in temperature, and, if properly packed, protect your back from the assaults of your water bottle. A light, fold-into-a-pocket rain jacket should also have a permanent place in your pack, as should a pair of soft, extra light moccasins, whose soles have neither been reinforced nor lined. Intended only as slippers, these last should never be used for walking, but kept clean and dry against the possibility of your wanting to put them on for an indoor lunch when your bare feet cannot otherwise be brought into an acceptable condition (or—much less likely, but reassuring to note—to keep an injured foot clean in an emergency).

You should, however, be able to get your feet clean enough for barefoot lunching if you also carry a small rag soaked in rubbing alcohol or surgical spirits and sealed into a sandwich bag. Alcohol does an excellent job of cleaning bare feet, and, according to some, also helps to toughen them. I must warn you that as it leaves the skin very dry and prone to cracking, its use should be avoided in winter unless followed immediately by an application of lotion or lanolin. You will also want to equip yourself with minimum first aid supplies (a small tin of bandage strips and some aspirin) and the essentials of woodcraft (maps, compass, pocket knife, and so on).

Get into the habit of carrying a litter bag. Not just for the frugal remains of your own repast, but so that you can pick up bits of trash that you might find along the trail. This should, for a barefoot hiker, be a matter of pride.

To return, for the moment, to the subject of preserving the integrity of your repast, you might consider packing it in a plastic container of such a sort as might prove useful if the opportunity for berry picking presented itself, as it often does in summer.

Dealing with Thorns

Enjoyable and rewarding as this activity is, it does force us to consider the somewhat less pleasant subject of thorns. Brambles are not usually present on forest trails and can generally be avoided. But when you cannot, or do not wish to avoid them, you should tread straight down on them with your now quite adequately toughened soles and thus avoid unsightly scratches on the much more vulnerable tops of your bare feet. If you do so properly, thorns embedding themselves in your soles will be a surprisingly rare occurrence. If you cannot conveniently extract them right away (or, more commonly, do not notice that you have acquired them, as you may have become accustomed to the much more typical but often indistinguishable sensation of their penetrating the skin only slightly and being drawn out again as you step off them), you can much more easily tease them out at the end of the day after thoroughly soaking and scrubbing your bare feet. You may, in fact, not notice their presence until the next time you wear shoes, but they are really nothing to worry about; just tease them out when convenient. A word of caution: If you cannot, with at least a fair degree of certainty, locate a foreign body by sight, you should be very circumspect about doing any "exploratory surgery" with a sterilized needle, since quite often the discomfort is caused not by a foreign object, but rather by some minor trauma. It may be better to be patient and watchful. The body's natural defenses will often encapsulate an intruding object in a tiny pocket of pus. At this point (two or three days after the invasion) you can usually tease it out very easily and painlessly, simply hastening, as it were, what would otherwise eventually be a natural expulsion. Squeeze out any remaining pus and apply some disinfectant. Remember that the above is written with reference to thorns and small wood splinters. Serious puncture wounds or cases of suspected toxicity should always be referred to a physician.

Pavement

If summer finds you going barefoot everywhere you should definitely count yourself among the blessed; but you should, in any case, avoid too many miles of pavement walking. Pavement is very hard on the soles as it wears them down without having the texture to stimulate them to thicken again. You can compensate for some pavement walking—perhaps ten or twenty miles a week—by doing more walking on more positively textured surfaces, such as forest trails or—if your bare feet have grown strong enough to take it in stride—gravel; but beyond a certain limit, you would be wearing down your soles faster than you could possibly build them up. The balls of your feet would become painfully tender and much more prone to injury and eventually you would be unable to walk. Besides being abrasive, pavement is unyielding and thus very tiring to walk on. If you are walking long distances, you should avoid pavement whenever possible, and if you must walk on it, walk on the least abrasive part of it. Be careful though of using an overgrown grassy verge as an alternative to the paved surface of a highway, as it can be full of glass and other litter.

Soles of Good Thickness

It is possible on the other hand, for your soles to get *too* thick, and thus become prone to cracking. Unfortunately, pavement walking is not a satisfactory answer to this problem as it will not tend to abrade those parts of the sole that most need abrading. Use coarse sandpaper to remove some of the excess in these areas (generally the edges of the heels). If you prefer to keep your soles extra thick as a hedge against the unknown demands of the sort of barefoot holiday that will be the subject of the next chapter, be sure to use an extra amount of lotion on them to keep them supple.

CHAPTER IX

Holiday Hiking:
New and Different Terrains

Setting Off Barefoot

Many of us, if fortunate enough to arrange extended holidays for ourselves, prefer to spend them in environments totally different from the ones where we spend most of our lives. Those who enjoy going barefoot also enjoy the idea of setting off on such excursions with our bags unburdened by shoes. You may thus be planning to set off sometime in late summer for a barefoot fortnight to be spent, at least in part, hiking on trails and terrains untypical of your previous experience.

Gravel-Toughened Soles

You will want your bare feet to be firm enough and strong enough to cope with a much more demanding schedule of hiking than they are currently accustomed to, and since they may have as well to deal with a good many miles of pavement or other abrasive surfaces, you will also want their soles to be as thick and tough as possible at the onset. An intensive, short-term, toughening program is, in this instance, quite appropriate.

Bare soles are best toughened by a strict and regular, but carefully measured, regimen of walking or running on surfaces which provide maximum texture with minimum abrasion, and the best such surface is gravel. Smooth pebbles are good but crushed stone is better. It should be fairly thickly bedded in earth, *not* lying thinly atop hard pavement. Start out with something like a half-inch grade, bedded deeply enough so that you can wriggle your toes into it. You should, if your feet have the sort of experience assumed in the previous chapter, find walking on this to be quite pleasant and very stimulating. Try to spend about twenty minutes each day walking, and—once you are sure the course is safe—running on this surface. Work up through coarser and coarser grades as your bare soles toughen.

When you can comfortably run barefoot on gravel of one grade, you are ready to progress to the next larger and coarser grade until—if you should advance so far in the two or three weeks that you should allow yourself for this preparation—you can run comfortably even on the largest and coarsest railway bed gravel. Walk or run up on your toes. Your heels probably do not need any more toughening and running on your toes will do more to firm and strengthen your muscles and tendons as well. While you are walking about on the gravel, you should practice picking up pebbles with your toes to make them strong and nimble enough to cope with any rock climbing or scrambling that you may want to do.

You will want those bare soles to be as firm, as tough, and as thick as you can get them—a good quarter of an inch thick over the balls of your feet—but be prepared to use prodigious amounts of lotion or lanolin (in earlier times, those who went barefoot were generally taught to use fat or oil) to keep them in proper condition. You do not want to develop layers of dead, dry, crack-prone callus, but smooth, supple soles of firm, yet flexible, *living* leather. Remember that you will be depending on your bare feet not only to take you wherever you want to go on your holiday, but to be totally presentable when you get there, and that you must therefore be willing to invest the time and attention in them to keep them at their best.

Appropriate Preparations

Please understand that I do not recommend this rather rigorous regimen except to those planning periods of very intense and sustained hiking activity on highly abrasive or otherwise punishing surfaces. Gravel-toughening is a short-term expedient with few if any long-term benefits; and although not nearly so uncomfortable as it might seem, it does require a good deal of discipline and takes up time that might otherwise be spent on much more enjoyable hiking. You will not need any special preparation if all you are planning is forest trail hiking with a few odd rock scrambles.

Most of this book has been concerned with woodland hiking. What follows is very general advice on hiking barefoot through some other types of terrain.

It is necessary, however, to preface these paragraphs with a few words of caution. General remarks concerning terrain types cannot possibly exhaust the list of cautions that must be observed in any specific environment. You must, as a holiday hiker, make every effort, as mentioned in Chapter VI, to thoroughly inform yourself concerning any special hazards peculiar to the area that you are visiting, so that you can exercise appropriate caution to avoid those hazards.

Fields and Fences

You may often find yourself using public rights of way across private agricultural land. Courtesy and respect for the rights of the landowners demand that you keep to the paths provided and that you carefully close behind you any gates that you open. Your safety as a barefoot hiker demands that you be extra watchful around stiles and fences—especially metal ones that have been abandoned. Stubs of former metal fence poles, just protruding through the ground, are very dangerous. If you see one of these, watch carefully for others which may be in line with it. You will note that this rule is repeated in the final summation—and with good reason: Often rusted to the color of the surrounding earth, and all too frequently found along the type of path here mentioned, they are among the most serious hazards to barefoot hikers. You must, in such areas, be especially mindful of their possible presence as you watch the ground in front of your feet. Watch also for nails and bits of wire, both on the ground and on whatever stiles and fences you find yourself climbing over. Remember that as a general rule, manmade objects are more dangerous than natural ones, so be especially watchful wherever men have altered the landscape.

Wetlands

Since we can, under the general title of wetlands, subsume all of the fens, swamps, marshes, bogs, beaver ponds, water meadows, and tidal flats the world over, it is obvious that we are discussing a great variety of environments with an equal variety of characteristics. Some are home to all sorts of unpleasant and often venomous and/or disease carrying life-forms, and some other hazards as well, such as quicksand, while others are harmless places where barefoot children come to catch minnows. Only someone with local knowledge can tell you which are which, and without such knowledge, it is best not to go wading in where you can not see the bottom upon which you will be standing. It is unlikely that you will set out to do any wetland hiking *per se*, but many woodland trails cross wetland areas and many nature centers intentionally include them to provide a greater diversity of mini environments. Wooden bridges are often provided in such places and these generally contain nails whereof barefoot hikers need to be watchful, especially when the bridges themselves have begun to rot and fall apart. A good, sturdy walking stick is very helpful both in this type of terrain, and on muddy bridle paths, as it can be used both to test the footing and, at times, virtually to vault over a bad patch, or at least to take a good part of your weight off your bare feet so that they do not sink as deeply.

Shorelines

A hike along a section of shoreline normally includes sandy beaches, rocky coasts, and perhaps some developed waterfront. Almost everyone goes barefoot in these areas, but that should not make you any less vigilant. More people mean more litter—and much of it is hazardous. Watch out also for protruding nails on boardwalks. Remember when you are scrambling on wet, slimy rocks, that they can be very treacherous— even under bare feet.

Stony Ground

In very stony areas, you will do best to try to walk on the larger stones, selecting one for each footfall and literally gripping it with your toes as you step on and off it. Your heels should not touch the ground at all at such times. When there are not enough of the larger stones to permit you to apply this technique, you will simply have to fall back on your preparation of walking barefoot on gravel and tough it out. Here again, stay on your toes. They are designed to be able to cope with such situations much better than your heels could. Remember that as long as you do not push yourself too far, the experience will ultimately toughen your soles all the more—so think positively and do not let the shod see you wincing. A good pair of strong, healthy, well-toughened bare feet should have little difficulty in coping with the equivalent of two or three miles of even the most punishing railway bed gravel in the course of a day's hiking in mild weather, but, as I shall explain more fully in Chapter XI, you must *never* subject your bare feet to any sort of rough ground in freezing or even near freezing temperatures.

Scrambling Up and Over Rocks

The fear that I encounter most often in those who are scrambling up and over rocks for the first time in their bare feet is that they will stub their toes. I always tell them that if they are *conscious* of their toes, and use them carefully and in ways that take full advantage of their sensitivity as well as their strength and flexibility, they will be no more likely to injure their toes than to injure their fingers, and will furthermore be able to cover this sort of terrain much more effectively in their bare feet than they could in shoes. This advice has always proven to be both reassuring and very effective. When scrambling up rocks on all fours, you should think of and use your bare feet as another pair of bare hands.

Having no experience myself of technical climbing, I would not presume to say anything on that subject save that if I were to take it up, I would insist on learning from an experienced *barefoot* climber.

Caverns

Cave *exploration* is another technical sport that one could only safely take up with an experienced companion. Caverns that have been professionally opened to (and prepared and lighted for) the public, however, are very interesting places to visit, and their cold floors can be quite pleasant under bare feet, particularly in summer.

An Apology

Because I feel that I would be violating an implicit trust if I were to attempt to advise the reader on aspects of hiking outside my own personal experience, there are a few terrain types (perhaps most notably desert terrains) that I have had to omit here in the hope that I might gain the experience necessary to include mention of them in future editions.

CHAPTER X

Autumn: Special Pleasures, Special Cautions

Barefoot Each Morning

Welcome as summer may have seemed when she arrived, if she has stayed long and been hot, you may well bless that first morning when the grass, laden with a heavy dew, imparts a decided chill to your bare feet, informing them in no uncertain terms that, like it or not, the seasons are changing. Summer will probably reassert herself later in the day, and you can expect that warmer and cooler mornings will chase each other across the calendar for some weeks, but as your bare feet bravely sample the cold carpet that was warm and verdant only yesterday, you ask yourself: "Winter? ...Barefoot?"

Yes, and when it comes you will probably enjoy it, but you will in fact have a long season to prepare for it. The best preparation that I can recommend is to take a short walk every morning—be it a dog walk, or a brief constitutional, or even just a quick run out to your trash cans, in your bare feet. Do this without fail whatever the weather. Take special care to note the temperature and the state of the ground. Come to terms with the changing weather *not* by making your-self indifferent to it, but by making yourself all the more acutely aware of it through the sensitivity of your bare soles. Do this faithfully and when the first frost, and later the first snow, arrive, you will find yourself stepping out to sample them with happy anticipation.

Enjoying Dry Leaves Safely

What comes the most to mind at autumn's mention are mountains of dry leaves. Take a walk in the woods on one of those delicious days when autumn deigns to step aside for a late Indian Summer and the leaves are several inches deep on the forest floor and let your bare feet feel them—sometimes crackling with all the crispness of the autumn air—sometimes whispering sensuously back to your bare soles with what seems a slightly soapy softness.

As these wind-wakened wraiths dance excitedly at the very approach of bare feet, and then settle se-ductively over the tops of your toes with every step, the temptation to shuffle through them can be over-whelming, but **NO, YOU MUST NOT.** You could be badly injured by running your bare feet across sharp stones or other objects hidden underneath them. For all the pleasure they promise to those who will walk upon them wisely, leaves are nonetheless a hazard to the heedless in that they obscure the forest floor from view and thus hide a multitude of potential dan-gers. Step lightly and straight down as always, and be very alert to what you feel under you now thoroughly sensitized soles. Be ready to retract a step if you do not like the feel of what you are stepping on.

Apples and Acorns and Nut Brown Soles

Acorns are counted among the worst annoyances of autumn by many barefoot hikers, not only for their often unwelcome feel underfoot but also for their most annoying habit of hitting hikers on the head. You might try turning them to your amusement though, by taking one up in your toes every so often and trying to see how far you can carry it along that way while walking.

Picking edible nuts—or apples, for that matter—is another autumn activity that you will find more fun in your bare feet, and a barefoot visit to a pick-your-own orchard can be a very enjoyable alternative to a hike.

One of the things that you may notice after a healthy amount of autumn hiking is that your bare soles are turning a rich nut brown. This is caused by the tannin in the leaves through a process much like that whereby leather is tanned. It is harmless and natural, and not at all unattractive for the few weeks that it lasts.

CHAPTER XI

Winter: Still Barefoot, Even in Snow

It is the evening of January 16, 1992 as I write this. It is a little after 11:00 P.M. and I have just returned from walking my dog behind the house. I had just arisen from a customary two hours of sleep to make myself a drink and begin an equally customary hour or so of reading, writing, and generally relaxing before retiring again for the rest of the night. Dressed for bed, as is my custom, in nightshirt and cap, I wrapped myself in a dressing gown, but of course went barefoot. I stood in perhaps half an inch of intensely cold, powdery snow, clenching and unclenching my hands around J.D.'s lead as I willed my bare feet to melt through it and down to the frozen earth. He took a very long piddle. Then I walked, very deliberately, back to my kitchen door and checked the temperature: 0°F. Stepping back inside, I dried both his feet and mine with a sense of satisfaction. I had not been out long enough to feel any pain from the cold, and certainly not long enough for it to have done me any harm—just long enough, in fact, to have thoroughly enjoyed it.

As I mentioned in the previous chapter, I keep myself to a strict rule (which I also recommend) of never letting a day or a night go by without taking at least a brief walk out of doors, barefoot on the bare ground. Shockingly Spartan as such a regimen might seem to those who might only contemplate it, this momentary exercise is intended primarily to awaken the senses rather than build endurance, but it does harden the soles and improve the circulation as well as build a sense of pride, pleasure, and confidence in being on terms with the elements.

Before going further, I must make two things quite clear: the first is that I would never consider actually *hiking* barefoot in such severe weather; and the second is that these are very extreme conditions for my part of Connecticut, occurring perhaps once or twice during the entire course of an average winter, and rarely lasting more than a day or so.

In this chapter, more than in any of the others, I feel it necessary to remind the reader that I am writing entirely from personal experience and that this is the experience of a middle aged man of British and Northern European descent, nonsmoking and in very good health, who has been a very avid and regular year-round barefoot hiker for more than twenty years now. Even more relevant here, however, is the fact that most of these twenty-odd years, and *all* of their winters, have found me either in Southern England or Southern New England. Although the Connecticut winters are on average the more severe, both climates are characterized by winters wherein a few short spells of freezing weather are interspersed with periods of much milder and occasionally decidedly warm weather, and—best of all for the barefoot hiker—it is very typical of both climates that a snowfall be followed immediately by a warm spell.

Melting Snow, the Ultimate Barefoot Pleasure

Melting snow on a fairly warm winter day is perhaps the most perfect pleasure that nature affords bare feet. Soft and sensuous, cool and cleansing, it is a sensation delicious in the same sense—though not to the same senses—as eating the very best sort of ice cream. Although the opportunity for this singular pleasure may present itself (at least in the climates that I am accustomed to) several times in the course of a single winter, it is quite ephemeral and rarely lasts more than a day. Thus it may, quite sadly, be a year or so before such a day coincides with one wherein you are so free of the constraints of clock and calendar that you can afford to leave both shoes and watch at home with an heart-felt "good riddance" as you set off for several miles of happy hiking. Nevertheless, even if you cannot afford your bare feet the whole of such a day, you should at least promise them some part of it, even if it be only a lunch hour taken at a park or a very brief visit to a nature center on your way home from running some errand.

Minding Your Overall Heat Economy

Although melting snow is all the more sensuous on one of those warm-enough-for-shirtsleeves days that here in Connecticut tend to arrive to relieve the chill at some time in the middle of most winters, you can enjoy this pleasure quite comfortably on any calm sunny day when the temperature is even a few degrees above freezing. The saying that "If your feet are cold, all of you is cold" is a half-truth wherein cause and effect are often confused. As long as the temperature is significantly above freezing, you need only concern yourself with your total heat economy. This is the result of the total amount of heat that your body is either producing through metabolism or gaining from sunlight absorbed by dark-colored clothing, balanced against the total amount of heat your body is losing either by general radiation, direct (and thus fairly rapid) transfer to the air from exposed parts, indirect (and therefore much slower) transfer to the air through layers of insulating clothing, and—now that you have chosen to leave them bare—conduction to the ground through the soles of your feet. In terms of your total heat economy then, you need simply offset the added heat loss you have incurred by renouncing whatever insulation shoes might have provided you by increasing the amount of insulating clothing, and thus reducing heat loss elsewhere on your body.

Remember also that your metabolism, and therefore the rate at which your body produces heat, is vastly increased by exercise. For this reason a number of layers of clothing which can be easily taken off and put on again are far more suitable for hiking than a single heavy coat.

Were this simple concept of a total heat economy the only thing that we needed ever consider, any of us could, in principle, dress warmly enough to allow us to afford bare feet even in Arctic cold. This is, however, unfortunately not the case, for each individual must also consider the efficiency of his or her circulatory system. This is something which, like metabolism, varies *enormously* and is determined by a number of health factors. It is only by the efficient circulation of warm blood that the body's core temperature can be maintained at the extremities. Regardless of how efficient our circulation might be, there would for each of us come a point at which the chilling effects of temperature, humidity, and wind became so severe that the temperature of bare feet could not be maintained at a safe level even if there were a surplus of heat building up in a well-insulated upper body.

I can say of *myself* that I can hike barefoot, in perfect comfort and with no ill effects, for any number of miles on a calm, sunny, 40°F day with a full inch of snow on the ground. Under all of the same conditions, excepting a calm air temperature of 30°F, I would still enjoy going barefoot, but would want to limit my walk to less than a mile and less than twenty minutes. At 20°F, I might only try a quarter of a mile and would not want to spend more than about five minutes in the snow. At these same temperatures but over dry ground, I would feel safe in attempting two or three times the above distances. I would consider high wind to be a very significant limiting factor and likewise any depth of snow beyond an inch or so.

The above would for me be the limits of comfort. YOUR OWN LIMITS WILL PROBABLY BE DIFFERENT FROM MINE, AND *YOU MUST APPROACH THEM WITH EXTREME CAUTION.* If you are in good health, however, and stay well on the cautious side of what I have indicated above, you will at least stay within the limits of safety.

Barefoot Gaiters

One way to keep your feet and legs warmer and more comfortable while continuing to enjoy the sensitivity of your bare soles is to equip yourself with a pair of *barefoot gaiters*. If you cannot get them ready made, a good leather crafter, such as you may have already had recourse to for moccasins or soleless sandals, can make them up for you quite inexpensively, or, if you like, you can try making some up for yourself according to the following pattern:

> **You will need** two strips of fairly soft, pliant leather, each approximately 12″ long (depending on foot size) and 2″ to 3″ wide, a glover's needle, a spool of waxed, rot-proof thread, and an awl or leather punch. These can be purchased anywhere that sells leather craft supplies. You will also need a pair of leg warmers. Fewer places carry these now than when they were a popular fashion item, but you should still be able to find them in a dancers' supply shop. If there is any choice, take a pair with well knit and well elasticized cuffs—preferably doubled

over cuffs or extra long cuffs that you can double over yourself.

Working barefoot, wrap the leather strips around your insteps and arches, as in the illustration. The softer, more textured sides should go against your skin and the harder, smoother sides should face out. The overlap on top of each foot should end up with its edge lying directly over the large metatarsal bone which runs up to the ankle from the big toe. Use a soft pencil to trace along this line on each foot so that you can properly align the leather for punching and sewing. Mark also for left and right.

Now remove the leather strips and realign them on a flat surface. With pencil and ruler, lay out a rectangle atop each whose sides are ¼″ in from the edges of the overlap. These will be your stitch lines. Place ticks along them to premark your punch holes at ¼″ intervals (more or less), but lay out the holes so that the total number of holes on each rectangle will be an *odd* number.

Now wrap each strip around a flat wooden block in exactly the same way that you had wrapped them around your bare feet. Using your bare toes to hold them down in strict alignment, punch each hole through both lapping layers with your awl or leather punch, and, if need be, a mallet. This will make the job of sewing much easier and safer. If you use an actual plug-removing punch you may even be able to sew with a dull bodkin rather than the very sharp and somewhat dangerous glover's needle.

When you begin sewing together each strip to form a stirrup, you should temporarily tape or otherwise secure the tail end of a 30″ thread onto the top side of the underlapping end of the leather strip so that when you are finished, it will be inside the closed pocket that the stitching will form. Pass the needle and thread down through the hole in the corner of the underlapping rectangle which will be most nearly over your big toe and back up through the next hole in the front edge. Then bring it up through the corresponding hole in the overlapping end of the leather strip. Continue with running stitches, over and under, stitching together the front edge of the lap pocket of the stirrup toward the corner which will be most nearly over your little toe. Now continue the stitches along the outside edge, the back edge and finally the inside edge of the rectangle and back to the starting point.

Having completed both stirrups to this point and fitted them back onto your bare feet, they should appear, more or less, like those in the illustration below. Most importantly, about 12" to 18" of thread

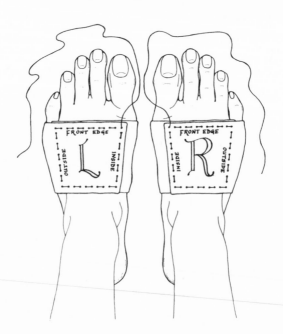

should be emerging from the top of each, at the hole marking that corner of the rectangle most nearly over your big toe.

Now it is time to fit the leg warmers. Unless you got them with the cuffs already sewn down double, you should choose the ends with the longest cuffs to be the ankle ends and as you put them on, double them under about 2″ towards your ankles so that the doubling does not show from the outside. You should begin the first stitch joining the now folded edge of each leg warmer to the front edge of each stirrup while they are still on your bare feet, pulling a point along that folded edge out over your big toe and passing the thread from the stirrup up through both layers of the fold about ¼″ back from its edge, and then back down again through both layers at a point about ¼″ (or the space of one knitting rib) along that edge towards your little toe and the same distance back from it.

Now carefully remove both the stirrups and the leg warmers from your bare feet and continue to stitch, passing the needle down through the second hole along the front edge of the stirrup from outside to inside and then continuing a line of running stitches joining the leg warmer to the stirrup until, looking at the inside of the front edge of the stirrup, you see that you have filled the spaces between the stitches that originally held the stirrup together with another set of stitches and the thread is now at the point that will be most nearly over your little toe when the completed gaiters are back on your bare feet. From the top, you should see the edge of the cuff fold of the leg warmer projecting just over the front edge of the stirrup and each stitch anchoring down one knitting rib (unless experimentation with the snugness of the cuff has led you to vary this formula).

Finally, stitch back along the same line of stitches toward the point that will be most nearly over your big toe. You may either use another line of running stitches to double up on those that originally held the stirrup together, or you may choose to do a spiraling overcast stitch over and along the folded edge of the leg warmer which only hooks under the tops of the original stitches and thereby tightens them. In either case, when you reach the original big toe corner again, you will want to push the needle into the closed pocket of the stirrup and back out the opposite corner so that you can bury the end of the thread alongside its beginning.

Worn in conjunction with a sturdy pair of trousers and either long johns or sweatpants, a good pair of barefoot gaiters will cover and insulate your insteps, arches, and ankles while allowing the most sensitive parts of your soles to remain bare. By sealing your trouser ends, you will retain most of the heat produced by your leg and calf muscles in the process of walking. This is for the benefit of your bare toes, which, being now only inches away from a very well insulated primary source of warmth, will be much easier for your circulatory system to serve. From my experience, I would say that the addition of barefoot gaiters and sweatpants should keep you about as comfortable at 35°F as you would be in trousers alone (with exactly the same upper body covering) at 45°F.

The leather stirrups of your barefoot gaiters will not be damaged by machine washing and drying. Hand lotion works well to relax and recondition the leather when dry.

Flexing Toes with Each Step

Another practice which will go far toward keeping bare toes warm in cold weather is to flex them with each step. Clench the toes of the trailing foot as it leaves the ground and clench them hard—so that you feel it in your calf muscles—before relaxing them again to step down. This will not only generate much more heat for you through increased muscular activity but will also result in a very significant quickening of your circulation.

The use of this technique at the start of a hike can markedly shorten the sometimes uncomfortably long warm-up period that your body needs to properly marshal its natural abilities to keep your bare feet warm in moderately cold weather.

Avoiding Blisters

Going barefoot in freezing weather is always a matter of how long, how far, and how much. There are of course, limits to the amount of any physical activity that the body can tolerate at any temperature; for reasons that I am not qualified to attempt to explain, as the temperature falls below the freezing point, there is a very sharp and sudden reduction in what flesh can withstand. There are indeed ways that we can extend the limits of our resistance to cold, but we can extend them only so far.

At freezing temperatures on dry ground, you might, with the help of your long johns and barefoot gaiters and all the advice that I have been able to provide, be able to safely hike barefoot for one or two miles, but only if the ground were not too rough and you avoided pavement and gravel entirely. Rough ground can easily blister very cold toes. I am referring here to a type of superficial hæmatoma or blood blister which appears first red and then black. Whether they should be seen as a simple example of mechanical injury, or as an early symptom of actual frost damage, I should not—having no claim to any medical knowledge—venture to say. I can, however, tell you from experience that if you are so imprudent as to incur them, you will find them on the pads of whichever of your toes tend to strike the ground with the greatest force, and you may well find yourself spending a week walking on your heels to avoid the pain of them.

The few times that I myself have had this very painful and annoying experience have all been the result of foolishly trying to keep pace with groups of shod hikers in freezing weather and, as I remember, very largely on pavement. Please take this warning and never put yourself in that position. In freezing weather, you should only take short walks, over leaf-softened forest trails, alone or with other barefoot hikers. Pay careful attention to the pads of your toes and if they begin either to lose sensitivity or show the least sign of trauma, turn back, and if you decide to retreat along a roadway, put on your moccasins. Leave your feet bare when you drive, so that your car heater can warm them.

Importance of Lotion

Feet, like hands, are subject to painful cracking when subjected to alternating wet cold and dry heat, and this is especially true of the fairly thick soles which, as a barefoot hiker, you will by now have developed.

Once started, cracks in your soles may prove very difficult to heal. You can prevent them, however, by applying a liberal amount of lotion or lanolin to your bare feet several times a day, but particularly before retiring, and especially generously before putting on socks and shoes, and, as mentioned in the summer chapter, keeping down any calluses. Try to find room in your day pack for a small towel and some lanolin, as these will be useful before, during, and after any barefoot hike that involves snow or cold water wading.

CHAPTER XII

Forming A Group or Chapter of Barefoot Hikers

Necessary Attributes of an Anchor Person

Every organization, especially at its inception, needs at least one individual with an unwavering commitment to doing everything in his power to promote its ends and ensure its success, and who is also willing and able to work comfortably and effectively with others. He must, among his other attributes, be free enough of personal pride to be constantly and actively seeking to recruit another of equal commitment who will be capable of replacing him, knowing that he could never be replaced by any committee of half-hearts, even if the sum of their talents were greater than his. As important as talent is, commitment is far more important. This unwavering commitment is no less necessary an attribute of anyone who would consider becoming the founder and anchor of a group or chapter of Barefoot Hikers. The other conditions which a barefoot hiker would need to meet to successfully undertake such a task would be:

- A genuine love of going barefoot outdoors lived out to the greatest extent possible in a barefoot lifestyle complemented by a happy, positive, and unselfconscious willingness to share the joy of going barefoot with others.

- At least a full year's experience as an avid barefoot hiker (at least fortnightly), including fairly intimate knowledge of at least half a dozen sections of local trail that would serve as suitable training grounds for first-time barefoot hikers.

- Residence in an area both sufficiently populous to give a good potential membership base and rural enough to include a fair number of good hiking areas all within easy driving distance.

- At least a four hour block of time that could be absolutely reserved for barefoot hiking at least twice a month and preferably at the same time each and every weekend.

Assuming that you have found yourself ready and willing to take on this task, let us further assume that you are starting the group with only one member—yourself—a perfectly appropriate beginning!

Time and Place

Your first order of business should be to select a regular meeting time which you both know to be convenient to yourself and can assume to be convenient to most of the general population.

Next, you will need to decide on a regular meeting place whence your group can carpool. It must be accessible, easily located, and have plenty of free parking. In view of the fact that you will be the anchor person of the group, it should also be as close as possible to your home.

Preparing a Standard Handout

You will now want to prepare a concise, single page, type-written handout, which will also serve as your standard press release. As a recognized affiliate of the Barefoot Hikers of Thomaston, Connecticut (a status that we are prepared to confer freely on any barefoot hiker who applies in writing) you will be both fully welcome and strongly encouraged to simply copy our standard handout (including its distinctive letterhead), blocking out the first and last paragraphs and substituting your own local particulars for ours. Whether you refer to the organization that you are founding as an affiliate or a chapter of the Thomaston-based organization, you will be asked to mention this affiliation, and doing so will provide you with an instant loan of continuity, credibility, and confidence.

You should not, at least at this early stage, make any attempt to publish any sort of schedule of where you will be hiking on what weekend, but rather take full advantage of the fact that you are able to make that decision on the day with regard to both the weather and the experience and schedule needs of those who actually show up for each hike. To facilitate your planning, you should make sure that your handout contains, as ours does, a strong request that all participants phone you beforehand.

Barefoot Hikers

Now an independent group, based in Thomaston, CT, we shall, weather permitting, meet each Saturday morning at 9:00 AM to car pool from the commuter parking lot on US 6 off exit 39 of Route 8 to continue the Barefoot Hiking Programme begun in coöperation with the Newtown Hikers and the Sierra Club with the <u>BAREFOOT ON THE MATTATUCK TRAIL</u> Series of 1989, which we are currently repeating.

We are an open group in the sense that anyone interested is more than welcome to participate in our programme and we expressly extend this welcome to children and well behaved dogs. As in the past, all new participants will be placed on our mailing list, and counted as members, but although it may in future be necessary to ask for voluntary contributions to offset postal expenses, no dues as such will ever be asked of anyone. Free and open as we are in this respect, however, we must nonetheless insist on certain rules:

First of all, we are <u>strictly barefoot</u>. We are committed to providing a full and competent programme of instruction to develop the sensitivity and awareness necessary for <u>safe</u> and enjoyable <u>Barefoot Hiking</u> and each new participant is provided with a copy of a carefully prepared booklet on <u>BAREFOOT HIKING</u>. In order to fulfill this commitment without distraction, we must insist that <u>everyone</u> go barefoot. Although we ordinarily recommend that shoes be left at home, first-timers may, if they feel more comfortable in doing so, <u>carry</u> some light footwear with them. Everyone, however, is expected to <u>arrive</u> <u>barefoot</u> and begin each hike in <u>bare feet</u>.

Everyone <u>must</u> bring <u>water</u> and should carry a rucksack or other bag, a light, fold-into-a-pocket waterproof and a lunch or snack depending on the length of the walk and the weather.

Because circumstances frequently force cancellations, <u>everyone</u> intending to participate <u>must</u> <u>phone</u> before each hike. The evening before is best but anytime before 8:30 AM on the Saturday in question will suffice. Please phone (203) 283-6594 in the evening or stop in at <u>Celebrations</u> card and gift shop, 89 Main Street, Thomaston, (283-9440) during business hours and ask for Richard.

You will need a great many copies of your handout, and if you do not have free access to a copying machine, the most important sort of a member for you to recruit at this stage might well be one who does. You will want to place small stacks of them in all of the libraries, nature centers, state parks, and public information centers in your area and perhaps also leave some with shopkeepers whom you know, and you will want to replenish these from time to time. You will want to keep some with you whenever you are hiking to give to those you might meet, and you will find yourself posting quite a few off to those who request more information after seeing newspaper notices. They will also serve as your press release sheets, and form the basis for such notices.

Press Relations

Good press relations are essential to the ends that you are trying to accomplish, and you will have to learn to cultivate them. You should begin by making a list of all the newspapers, large and small, that are published within about twenty miles of your home. Make phone calls to the offices of each, asking to speak with the person responsible for listing upcoming local events. Tell them that you wish them to carry a brief weekly notice of the regular meetings of a hiking group, and ask, in light of the fact that the notice will be unchanging, how often you should resubmit your press release—or, if possible, phone them—in order to ensure that the notice will appear continually. Each paper will probably have a different policy which you must carefully note on your list. Ask also to whose attention you should send your press release and note this as well, beside the name and address of each newspaper. Now you can post off a copy of your press release to each with a brief hand-written note on the margin asking that they print a brief weekly notice of your hikes. Newspapers generally make no charge to carry such notices and are happy to have them. They are considered as news.

Be sure to check the various papers in the weeks that follow to find out what they have made of your press release. In some cases, you may be disappointed to find no mention of it at all, but this is probably an oversight and not a reason to give up on that particular paper. It is far more likely that you will be quite pleasantly surprised to find that a newspaper has printed virtually the whole of your press release the first week and only subsequently reduced it to the brief mention that you had politely suggested. Whatever is printed, however, be sure that you check it for accuracy, particularly with regard to street names and telephone numbers, and let the editors know immediately if there is anything amiss.

Organizing, as you almost surely will be, the first barefoot hiking group in your area, it is very likely that you will eventually have a journalist asking you for an interview for a feature story. This is the most valuable kind of publicity that you can have. You must make it clear, however, that you have a strict policy of only granting interviews within the context of a reporter going along on a hike with you as a participant and very definitely in *bare feet* and that this applies to photographers and other sorts of assistants as well. Journalists tend to respect those who insist on setting out the terms under which they will be interviewed. They only dislike those who presume to tell them what to write. All you are trying to ensure is that whatever is written will be based on real, first person experience.

Let me share with you here one of my own most favorable experiences with the press.

Shoeless in the Forest

Liz Halloran, the reporter in charge of the Thomaston office of the *Waterbury Republican-American*, phoned me one morning in early September with a request for an interview. She had seen the notices of our Saturday morning walks and wanted to do a feature story on barefoot hiking. Finding that she could not easily make one of our regular walks, I offered to accommodate her schedule by taking her on a brief walk along one of my favorite sections of trail on a Thursday morning if she would return this courtesy by arriving in her bare feet. She instantly agreed and seemed quite comfortable and happy with the idea.

However, when the day arrived I was quite surprised to learn that the feet that she bared without the least hesitation to what I knew many would have feared as unknown hazards, and which appeared to pad quite happily across the gravel to the start of the trail, had never gone bare before. This, she assured me, was no mere matter of habit or happenstance. Her soles were soft and she intended to keep them that way. She had permitted them to go bare on this one very exceptional excursion but she would *not* be permitting them to go bare again, at least not, she allowed, until she found the time to take another walk with the Barefoot Hikers. I felt honored, but also somewhat sobered by the trust she was placing in me. I was also somewhat concerned that with notepad and pencil in hand, she was placing all the more trust in her untried toes to manage whatever scrambles lay ahead—but she brushed off that concern with a flourish of professional pride: These were the tools of her trade! Well...I did not want to be misquoted.

I need not have worried. Like some charmed tourist taking intense pleasure in all the peculiarities of a totally foreign country, this soft-soled guest from the shod world managed to totally enjoy her brief visit to the world of bare feet.

I would never have thought that the ninety minutes that Liz spent with me would have been enough to awaken her to the pleasures she described so well in her article. Many who had so sheltered their soles would have needed a good part of that time just to get past their sense of alarm, much less to learn the sense of joy that their sensitivity promised.

As much as this had surprised me, the very positive response that I received from her excellent article more than proved my guess that a bit of extra trouble to accommodate the press might be very well rewarded.

Shoeless in the forest, hikers discover a world of unexpected sensations

Waterbury Republican-American, Sunday, September 15, 1991, Waterbury, Connecticut
By Liz Halloran

THOMASTON—The cool mud squished through the toes of my bare feet.

Moments later, I padded softly over a carpet of dried pine needles and leaves, along a barely-moving stream. Watching the forest floor, I moved up a gentle hill, my woodland path now sprinkled with shiny, glinting mica and sharp acorn shells.

It was a quiet morning on the Mattatuck Trail; the zooming traffic of nearby Route 109 was a muffled buzz. It was my first experience barefoot hiking.

My guide and teacher, Richard Frazine, led the way at a brisk pace. A barefoot hiker for almost 20 years and a Mattatuck Trail regular, he pointed out potential hazards while keeping up a steady stream of suggestions for safe hiking without the benefit of socks and shoes.

"You must choose each footfall," he said, as we crossed a stream, picking our way through mossy rocks and cold water. "An-ticipate each step. If you kick, shuffle or drag your feet, your chance of injury multiplies enormously."

A barefoot hiker must step straight down, molding the foot to the ground so it "takes the shape of the earth," practically eliminating the chance of foot injury, Frazine said.

His toes curled around a rock so he could feel the chill and damp of the especially dense form of quartz. "It's holding the cool of the night," he said.

Why barefoot hiking? Why not stomp through the woods wearing a warm pair of scratchy wool socks and sturdy boots?

"There's a whole world on the forest floor," Frazine said. Going barefoot allows you to explore things with your feet — which, he says, are as sensitive as your hands.

He encouraged me to wriggle my toes through the moss and lichen that decorate rocks and tree trunks, to brush my foot over a mushroom the size of a saucer, to tickle my soles with high club moss, an archaic plant that looks like a tiny ground pine.

Frazine, who proudly says he's

got a "quarter inch of leather" on the bottom of his feet, acknowledges that the idea of traipsing through the woods barefoot frightens some and makes others nervous. Actually, he admits, that's how he felt when he first contemplated going unshod.

"I thought it would somehow strip me of being civilized, being human," Frazine said. "It's something bears do."

But once a woman friend convinced him of the pleasures of barefoot hiking, he was a convert. "It's something I enjoy tremendously," Frazine said as he ducked under a fallen tree and pointed out some Virginia creeper growing just off the trail.

He encouraged me to use my feet to "calibrate my senses" and to notice how a bare foot leaves almost no imprint on nature. We clambered up a small waterfall blanketed in moss that Frazine described as looking and feeling like a "shag carpet being continually washed."

As we pulled ourselves onto a large boulder at the side of the fall, Frazine talked about his family—wife, Joanne, and children, Beth, 6, and Charlie, 3.

The Frazines always walk barefoot in their High Street home, where they've lived for about four years. One of their favorite experiences is waiting for a winter thaw. When the air turns warm and the snow is melting—now that's a particularly pleasant barefoot walk, he said.

As we followed the trail back to our car, Frazine talked about how he's trying to share the experience of barefoot hiking. He's been extending a standing invitation to those who'd like to try a barefoot hike.

Each Saturday at 9 A.M., weather permitting, he meets interested hoofers at the commuter parking lot on Route 6 and exit 39 of Route 8 and takes them for a walk in the woods.

The dangers appear few and are usually confined to areas around public roads, where man's influence can be seen.

But walking deeper into the woods is "probably safer than going barefoot on public beaches," he said.

I know I came out of the experience a little dirty, but pleased and intrigued and unscathed.

I'd do it again.

Finding a Promotional Sponsor

You may have noticed that the sample handout of the Barefoot Hikers of Thomaston mentions a card and gift shop. As the managing partner in this business at the time of the group's founding, I had the advantage of being able to give it a perfect promotional sponsor. Even if you are not in such a position yourself, you should have little difficulty in finding a local business willing to make a mutually beneficial promotional arrangement with a group such as the one you are founding. The owner should definitely be a member of your group, but need not be more than an occasional participant as long as he has an enthusiasm that he can share with customers who ask about the handouts on his counter. The relationship should be warm, friendly, and mutually supportive.

T-Shirts and Sweatshirts

Small local businesses sponsor many nonprofit activities—especially local sports teams. The business typically contributes uniforms and equipment and the team carries its name. You will not need any equipment, and your "uniforms" will only consist of T-shirts and sweatshirts. Get together with your sponsor and shop around for the best deal on iron-on transfers for both your logo and your sponsor's. You will typically find that there is an initial screening and set up charge as well as a charge for each transfer printed. A transfer is normally about 12" × 12". Arrange your artwork so that each can be cut up to provide logos for at least two shirts—preferably one adult and one child size—if not more. Do not invest in an inventory of shirts, but buy them in the correct sizes as you need them for members and apply the transfers to them yourself. You probably will, however, find it economical to invest in a reasonable stock of transfers.

You should, along with your sponsor, consider getting involved in various community projects along with other types of groups. Participation in sponsored walks is a good idea; as is extending a standing offer to an organization for the blind to help facilitate their members participating in your walks.

Insisting on Bare Feet

You should try to widen your net, so to speak, in as many ways as you can, but be careful that you do not compromise your primary purpose of providing a program of instruction in safe and enjoyable barefoot hiking. I would urge you to do everything that you can to accommodate children, dogs, the handicapped, those who need help with transportation, and even those who may ask you to make special accommodations to their schedules; but I would warn you that you cannot afford to accommodate anyone asking for the option of going along as a shod observer rather than as a barefooted participant. What such persons are saying to you is that they are unwilling to support you in your instructional program. In accommodating them, you would be placing yourself in the position of an instructor who, lacking to begin with the disciplinary advantages of a classroom situation, must in addition put up with the presence of idly curious or simply disinterested nonstudents continually interacting with the legitimate members of his class. This is an entirely untenable position, and you must simply not permit yourself to be placed in it.

When people telephone in response to your newspaper notices, you will very often find that they managed either not to hear the word "barefoot" or assume it was just a word chosen to sound pleasantly quaint. The truth, when they finally learn it from you, will be far more often simply surprising than actually off-putting. This is the point at which you must be firm and truthful yet encouraging and enthusiastic. The best form of words might be something like:

"We hike in our bare feet, and we're committed to providing a program of instruction in barefoot hiking and, for that reason, we do have to insist that you arrive barefoot and at least begin the walk in your bare feet. We know some people are a bit uneasy about this the first time and if you are, we don't mind if you *carry* some light footwear with you if it makes you feel more at ease to do so. You would be better off though, if you saved yourself the weight and just left them at home. You won't need them. We always make sure we pick a nice, soft, easy trail if we have anyone along with especially soft soles, and our entire emphasis is on safety. It really is a lot of fun. I know you'll enjoy it. Everyone who comes along always does... All right then! We'll see you in the parking lot—in your bare feet!"

It should always be on the telephone, and not at the trailhead, that you make it clear that you expect everyone to set off barefoot. The only exception that I would ever make to the rule regarding bare feet would be in the case of a barefoot hiker bringing a companion constrained against going barefoot by a specific medical condition.

Building Confidence, Enthusiasm, and Membership

Remember that most of those who come out with you for the first time will not have read this book. Make sure you are well enough prepared to talk through all of the safety rules with them as you go along and to use your own bare feet not only to demonstrate those rules but also to point out to them the various hazards that may be found along the way. Their confidence in you will grow as they see that your first concern is for their safety. Get them to tell you how much they have gone barefoot in the past and how they feel about going barefoot, and be sure that you examine their bare soles. Remember that yours are likely to be much better toughened and far more experienced than theirs are. Try both to imagine how the ground might feel to a pair of bare soles much softer than yours, and find out from your first time barefoot hikers what it feels like to theirs. Look for ways to encourage them to develop their sensitivity and always stress the link between sensitivity and safety.

Be sure to thank everyone afterwards for their company and their support, and tell them that you would enjoy having them along again. Make sure everyone is provided with a copy of your handout and provides you with mailing list information. You should, through your sponsor, be able to provide everyone with T-shirts at no cost and sweatshirts at a very modest cost. Building enthusiasm builds membership.

A Personal Invitation from the Author

Since I began writing this book, it has been my ultimate hope that others, living beyond the tread of my bare feet, but sharing, nonetheless, my love of barefoot hiking, might join with me in setting up a support network, which, though far flung at first, might become more dense with time. Those few who find themselves blessed with the time and ability to found fully functioning chapters will be a blessing to all of us, but I would not want any to suppose that they could not be very welcome contributors to such a network just because their circumstances constrained them from making such ambitious commitments. I would like to make known that I offer my advice, my support, my friendship, and whatever reasonable assistance may be within my power to any and all barefoot hikers who might wish to contact me, whether it be for help in setting up chapters or simply to let me know that they are out there.

> Barefoot Hikers
> ℅ Richard Keith Frazine
> 50 Leigh Avenue
> Thomaston, CT 06787

SUMMATION

Hiking Barefoot Safely:
Ten Brief Rules

1. Always step *straight down!* Never allow your bare feet to kick, shuffle, or drag along the ground. This is more important than all the other rules together. It may require some conscious effort at first.

2. Always watch the path ahead of you. Learn to keep your eyes on the path a few yards ahead and pick the spot for each footfall a few paces ahead.

3. Try to keep your weight on the balls of your feet and not on your heels.

4. Never forget that you are going barefoot. Always devote a part of your attention to the soles of your bare feet.

5. Try to walk barefoot on as many different things as possible to sensitize your bare soles. A well developed sense of touch is very important both for safety and enjoyment. You must *consciously* work on developing this sense.

6. Be especially careful when you cannot clearly see the ground itself because of grass, leaves, and snow. Step lightly and carefully under these conditions and be prepared to retract a step if you don't like the feel of what you are stepping on. *Never run barefoot* unless you can both see the ground surface and have walked over it before.

7. Be especially careful at stiles and fences—especially metal ones that have been abandoned. Stubs of former metal fence posts just protruding through the ground are very dangerous. If you see one of these, watch carefully for others which may be in line with it.

8. By all means, try walking barefoot in snow—it is extremely pleasant, but only if it is no more than an inch or so deep and melting.

9. You can walk barefoot on dry ground in freezing weather, but never past the point where your feet become numb and never for more than one or two miles, especially on rough ground which is many times more punishing to cold soles than to warm.

10. Once properly conditioned, your bare feet will give you a great deal of pleasure, but only if you care for them. Bathe them and remove any small thorns after each hike, rub them each day with oil, lotion, or lanolin—especially in winter. Take the time to keep them in the very best condition and take *pride* in them.

Notes

Notes

Notes

Notes

Notes

Notes